From Continuous to Discrete

Integer Equations, Difference Equations, and Digital Electronics

First Edition (Republished)

Dean Banerjee

@2023 Dean Banerjee

All Rights Reserved.

ISBN: 978-1-312-28004-5

No part of this publication may be reproduced, stored in a retrieval system, or transmitted in any form or by any means, electronic, mechanical, photocopying, recording, or otherwise, without the written permission of the author.

From Continuous to Discrete

Integer Equations, Difference Equations, and Digital Electronics

Dean Banerjee

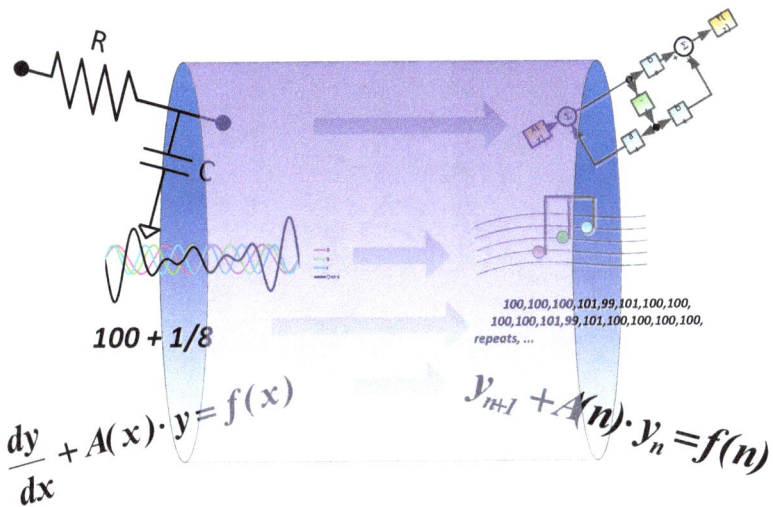

"God created everything by weight, number, and measure."

- Sir Isaac Newton

To my wife, Nancy, and my children, Caleb, Olivia, and Anabelle.

Preface

It takes a considerable amount of time and effort to learn valuable analog concepts that give understanding to the world around us. Among these concepts are algebra, differential equations, and analog electronics. These concepts can be used as a foundation to better understand the analogous discrete concepts of integer equations, difference equations, and digital electronics. This book has a main section devoted to each one of these three topics. These sections are fairly independent from one another, so the reader can skip any one of these if they are not of interest.

The first section expands on a foundation of algebra to understand modular and integer equations. Although modular arithmetic is not commonly taught in many schools, it has many interesting applications and it is not very difficult to understand some of the fundamental principles. There is an entire chapter devoted to the mathematical foundations and elegance of music theory which includes concepts such as harmony, chords, scales, and key signatures. Integer equations also have many practical applications and are interesting because they are possible to solve for more than one unknown with just a single equation.

The second section expands closed form solution methods for differential equations to difference equations. Differential equations are based on derivatives and difference equations are based on finite differences and this leads to similarities with some of the solution methods. By reading this section, the reader can simultaneously refresh their background in differential equations while also expanding this to understanding difference equations. Computers and numerical method definitely have their time and place with difference equations, so the last chapter is more focused on numerical methods for cases where a closed form solution is very cumbersome or cannot be found at all.

The third section focuses on digital electronics, including concepts such as Z transforms, analog to digital conversion, digital filters, and digital communications. These topics are all very involved covering each one in complete detail is not possible by only devoting a single chapter to each one, as is done in this book. That being said, it is still possible to highlight the key principles and relate these topics back to their analog counterparts.

This book has some fundamental theorems and derivations, but has a stronger emphasis on practical applications and solution methods. I would like to thank Miles Bennett for his assistance in correcting some of the mathematical errors in this book. I hope that you enjoy this book and gain a better understanding and appreciation of the many digital and discrete phenomenon in our world today.

Table of Contents

FROM ALGEBRAIC EQUATIONS TO INTEGER EQUATIONS
FUNDAMENTALS OF DISCRETE ARITHMETIC	3
APPLICATIONS OF THE MODULUS OPERATOR	10
LINEAR MODULUS EQUATIONS OF ONE VARIABLE	19
INTEGER ARITHMETIC APPLICATIONS TO MUSIC THEORY	30
HIGHER ORDER MODULUS EQUATIONS	39
DIOPHANTINE EQUATIONS	45

FROM DIFFERENTIAL EQUATIONS TO DIFFERENCE EQUATIONS
FINITE DIFFERENCES, SUMS, AND PRODUCTS	59
FIRST ORDER DIFFERENCE EQUATIONS	67
METHODS FOR HIGHER ORDER DIFFERENCE EQUATIONS	71
SYSTEMS OF ORDINARY DIFFERENCE EQUATIONS	79
OTHER TOPICS IN DIFFERENCE EQUATIONS	88

FROM ANALOG ELECTRONICS TO DIGITAL ELECTRONICS
THE DISCRETE Z TRANSFORM	99
CONVERTING BETWEEN ANALOG AND DIGITAL SIGNALS	107
DIGITAL FILTERS	117
DIGITAL COMMUNICATIONS	129

APPENDIX
TABLE OF SYMBOLS	141
GLOSSARY	142
INDEX	153

From Algebraic Equations to Integer Equations

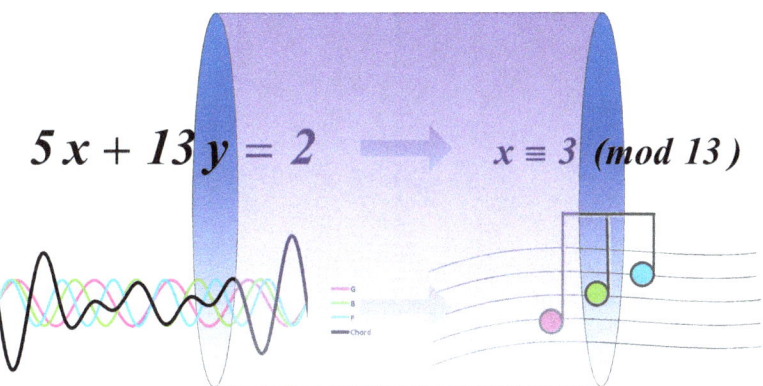

Chapter 1

Fundamentals of Discrete Arithmetic

Introduction

Discrete arithmetic is the mathematics of numbers which are defined only at specific values. Common examples might be the set of *whole numbers* such as 0,1,2, ..., or the set of *integers* such as ..., –3, –2, –1, 0, 1, 2, 3. The whole numbers and integers are both examples of an *evenly spaced set*, which is defined as a set of numbers where the space between each value and the next closest value is a constant. Another example of an evenly spaced set might be a set such as ... – ¼ , – ½ , 0, ¼, ½ ... ,which has a spacing of ¼.

Integer equations mostly deal with just integers, but the concepts involving integer arithmetic can be expanded to any evenly spaced set. For example, a problem involving numbers not in whole dollar amounts could be expressed in terms of cents and then all the theory regarding integer equations could be applied.

This chapter goes through some of the basic concepts for discrete arithmetic such as divisibility rules, greatest common divisor, least common multiple, and the modulus operator.

Divisibility Rules

The following rules are often useful in checking to see if one number is divisible by another.

Divide	Divisibility Rule	Example
2	The last digit is divisible by 2.	23478 is divisible by 2 because 8 is even.
3	The sum of the digits is divisible by 3.	23172 is divisible by 3 because 2+3+1+7+2 = 15, which is divisible by 3.
4	The last two digits are divisible by 4.	2978 is divisible by 4 because 78 is divisible by 4.
5	The last digit is 5 or 0.	23415 is divisible by 5 because it ends in a 5.
6	Use the divide rules for 2 and 3	23526 is divisible by 6 because it is divisible by 2 and 3.
7	There is no special rule , but you can subtract away multiples of 1001, which is a multiple of 7.	235319 is divisible by 7 because if we subtract away 235x1001, we get 319–235 = 84, which is divisible by 7.
8	The last 3 digits are divisible by 8.	2345464 is divisible by 8 because 464 is divisible by 8.
9	The sum of the digits is divisible by 9.	23627736 is divisible by 9 because 2+3+6+2+7+7+3+6 = 36, which is divisible by 9.
10	The last digit is a 0.	23531340 is divisible by 10 because it ends in 0.
11	The sum of the even digits minus the sum of the odd digits is divisible by 11	26334 is divisible by 11 because (2+3+4) – (6+3) = 0, which is divisible by 11.

Table 1-3   *Divisibility Checks for Numbers*

Prime and Relatively Prime

A *prime* number is a whole number one that is only divisible by itself and one. For example, 41 is considered to be a prime number. A collection of numbers is said to be relatively prime if they have no common factors other than one. An example of relatively prime numbers would be 39 and 100.

Greatest Common Divisor (GCD)

The greatest common divisor of two or more numbers is the greatest number that divides into all of them. To find this, the technique is to factor both numbers so that all common factors are known. Then the greatest common divisor is the multiple of all these common factors. For example, to find the greatest common divisor of 105 and 252 we could first factor them.

$$105 = 3 \cdot 7 \cdot 5$$
$$252 = 3 \cdot 7 \cdot 12 \quad (1.1)$$

The only shared factors are 3 and 7. It therefore follows that the greatest common divisor is the product of the numbers, which is 21. The factor of 12 in 252 could be reduced further, but this is unnecessary because it is relatively prime to the remaining factor of 5 in 105. Although this method is intuitive and simple, there is another technique called the Euclidean Algorithm that is faster and more efficient.

The Euclidean Algorithm for Greatest Common Divisor

The *Euclidean Algorithm* was first outlined in Euclid's *Elements* and gives an alternate way to calculate the greatest common divisor of two numbers. The basic concept is that since the greatest common divisor divides both numbers, it also divides the difference of these two numbers. By continually applying this principle, the problem of finding the GCD of two numbers can ultimately reduce the problem to just two numbers that are the same or where one is a multiple of the other. For instance, the following table shows that GCD(65, 143) =13.

Iteration	a	b	Difference
1	65	143	78
2	65	78	13
3	65	13	52
4	52	13	39
5	39	13	26
6	26	13	13
7	13	13	0

Table 1-4 Euclidean Algorithm Example

To make this process even faster, one can subtract higher multiples of the smaller number from the bigger one to reduce the number of steps. Below shows this concept being applied to GCD(65, 143) to find the result of 13.

Iteration	a	b	c
1	65	143	143 − 2 × 65 = 13
2	65	13	65 − 5 × 13 = 0

Table 1-5 *Faster Euclidean Algorithm Example*

Extending the of Greatest Common Divisor to Non-Integers

The concept of greatest common divisor (GCD) can be expanded to any finite set of numbers, provided that these numbers are related to each other by some rational number. For instance GCD(1/2, 3/4) = ¼ and GCD(2π, 5π) = π. However, GCD(3, 5π) is not defined because there exists no number that is in integer multiple of these two numbers.

There are two approaches to find the GCD in situations when it might not be so obvious by inspection. The Euclidean method is one method that is often effective if both numbers are non-repeating decimals. Table 1-6 shows how this method can be used to calculate GCD(19.68, 491.52).

Iteration	a	b	c
1	491.52	19.68	491.52 − 20 × 19.68 = 97.92
2	97.92	19.68	97.92 − 5 × 19.68 = − 0.48
3	19.68	0.48	19.68 − 40 × 0.48 = 0

Table 1-6 *Non-Integer Euclidean Algorithm Example*

It therefore follows from these calculations that GCD(19.68, 491.52) = 0.48. One useful shortcut used in this example was to allow for negative numbers. The reasoning is that because −0.48 divides both numbers, then so must +0.48. There are many different variations of the way that this method could be applied. For instance, the same result could also be found by finding GCD(1968, 49152) and then dividing the result by 100.

The above approach works well when the numbers involved can easily be expressed as terminating decimals. For situations involving rational numbers that are easier to express as fractions than decimals, there is another method that can be used. This method first starts with finding two integers, k_1 and k_2, such that:

$$GCD\left(\frac{a}{b},\frac{c}{d}\right) \cdot k_1 = \frac{a}{b}$$
$$GCD\left(\frac{a}{b},\frac{c}{d}\right) \cdot k_2 = \frac{c}{d}$$

(1.2)

These equations can be divided to yield:

$$\frac{k_1}{k_2} = \frac{a}{b} \cdot \frac{d}{c} \tag{1.3}$$

The expression can be reduced to a lowest terms fraction. Once k_1 is known, then the greatest common divisor can be calculated. For example, consider the following example

$$GCD\left(\frac{1}{15}, \frac{4}{35}\right) \tag{1.4}$$

For this, we first calculate the ratio:

$$\frac{k_1}{k_2} = \frac{1}{15} \cdot \frac{35}{4} = \frac{7}{12} \tag{1.5}$$

It therefore follows that:

$$GCD\left(\frac{1}{15}, \frac{4}{35}\right) \cdot 7 = \frac{1}{15}$$
$$\Rightarrow GCD\left(\frac{1}{15}, \frac{4}{35}\right) = \frac{1}{7 \cdot 15} = \frac{1}{105} \tag{1.6}$$

Least Common Multiple (LCM)

The *Least Common Multiple* (LCM) is defined as the smallest number that is a multiple of two or more numbers. For instance, the least common multiple of 35 and 14 is 70. In order to find this, one method is to factor both numbers to the point that they have no common factors. Then take the product of both of these factored forms, except when there is a shared factor, only count it once. For example, the least common multiple of 26 and 36 is the product of all the factors needed of these numbers, which would be $2 \cdot 12 \cdot 13 = 312$.

$$26 = 2 \cdot 13$$
$$36 = 2 \cdot 12 \tag{1.7}$$

An alternative method is to divide the product of the numbers by the GCD. For instance:

$$LCM(26, 36) = \frac{26 \cdot 36}{GCD(26, 36)} = \frac{26 \cdot 36}{2} = 312 \tag{1.8}$$

Expanding the Least Common Multiple to Non-Integers

The concept of least common multiple can be expanded to any evenly spaced set. For instance, to find what length was both a multiple of 3 ½ feet and 3 ¼ feet, the problem could be expressed inches as finding the greatest common multiple of 42 inches and 39 inches, which is 546 inches, or 45 ½ feet. Even if there was no such thing as inches, one could have done this problem in increments of ¼ feet.

LCM Application Example

Many clock generators generate multiple frequencies by generating a single frequency and dividing it down by integer values to get the desired result. Consider the following case where one wants to generate 12.288 MHz, 15.36 MHz, and 81.92 MHz from a single frequency, x.

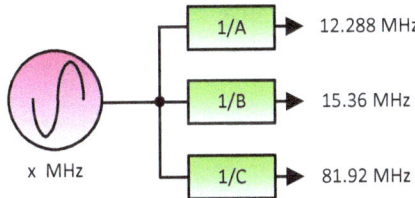

Figure 1-1 Clock Generator Example

One can reason that x must be a multiple of all three required frequencies and is therefore a multiple of the least common multiple of the three.

$$x = k \cdot LCM(12.288,\ 15.36,\ 81.92)$$
$$k = 1, 2, 3, \ldots \quad (1.9)$$

To find the result of (1.9), one can pull out common factors to reduce the problem.

$$\begin{aligned}
LCM(12.288, 15.36, 81.92) &= 0.001 \times LCM(12288, 15360, 81920) \\
&= 0.004 \times LCM(3072, 3840, 20480) = 0.032 \times LCM(384, 480, 2560) \\
&= 1.024 \times LCM(12, 15, 80) = 1.024 \times (3 \times 4 \times 5 \times 4) \\
&= 245.76
\end{aligned} \quad (1.10)$$

It therefore follows that the single frequency, x, needs to be a multiple of 245.76 MHz. Practical considerations specific to this application might help determine which multiple is most appropriate. For instance, if odd divide values were more difficult to implement, then using twice this frequency might work as shown in Figure 1-2.

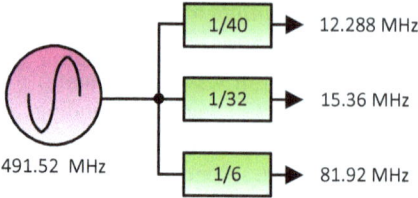

Figure 1-2   *One Possible Clock Generator Solution*

In the previous example, it was obvious that 0.001 divided all three frequencies, but there are other problems where it might not as easy to see what increment divides all numbers. In order to find the LCM in this situation, first take any two of the numbers and divide out any obvious numbers that factor them both, especially irrational numbers. After this is done, we are left with two rational numbers **a/b** and **c/d**. In order to find the least common multiple, we seek two integers, k_1 and k_2, such that:

$$\frac{a}{b} \cdot k_1 = LCM\left(\frac{a}{b}, \frac{c}{d}\right)$$
$$\frac{c}{d} \cdot k_2 = LCM\left(\frac{a}{b}, \frac{c}{d}\right)$$
(1.11)

These equations can be divided to yield:

$$\frac{k_1}{k_2} = \frac{b \cdot c}{a \cdot d}$$
(1.12)

Now the expression on the right hand side is a fraction and can be reduced to lowest terms. Then k_1 is simply the numerator. Once k_1 is known, the least common multiple can be easily found. If there are more than two numbers, taking the resulting LCM is found and repeat the process using this and one of the unused numbers until the LCM for numbers is found.

Example
In order to find the least common multiple of 1/6, 1/3, and 4/7, one can first LCM(1/6,1/3) = 1/3. After that, the following steps can be used to find LCM(1/3, 4/7).

$$\frac{k_1}{k_2} = \frac{3}{1} \cdot \frac{4}{7} = \frac{12}{7}$$
$$\Rightarrow k_1 = 12 \tag{1.13}$$
$$\Rightarrow LCM\left(\frac{1}{3}, \frac{4}{7}\right) = 12 \cdot \frac{1}{3} = 4$$

As a check, observe that 1, 1/3, and 4/7 all divide evenly into 4.

Modulus (mod) Operator

The notation $A \bmod M$ means to find the remainder of A when divided by M. If A happens to be negative, then one adds multiples of M until the result is positive or zero. For example, $5 \bmod 3 = 2$ and $-23 \bmod 5 = 2$. *Equivalence classes* refer to integers that have the same value modulus M. For instance, if $A \bmod M = 2$ and $B \bmod M = 2$, we could claim that $A \equiv B \equiv 2 \ (mod \ M)$. The following chapter goes through several applications of the modulus operator and many of the chapters to follow deal with solving equations with this operator.

Conclusion

This chapter has covered some of the basic concepts of different number sets and expanded some concepts such as least common multiple and greatest common divisor.

Chapter 2

Applications of the Modulus Operator

Introduction

The modulus operator is useful in solving integer equations as well as having many interesting applications. This chapter focuses on some interesting examples where the modulus operator can add some insight, starting off with modulo 2 and working up.

Modulo 2 Applications

Parity Check

A parity check is sometimes used to confirm that a message has been properly received. When sending a message that is a sequence of 1's and 0's the concept is to add one bit at the end that is either 1 or 0 such that when the whole message plus the additional bit all add up to an even number. Then at the receiving end, if the sum is not even, it is known that there is a communication error and the request can be made to resend the message. If there happened to be an even amount of errors, the parity check would be fooled, but if it is assumed that the error rate is relatively low, then this simple parity check would catch the majority of the errors.

Proof that Square Root of 2 is Irrational

The concept of even and odd (which is modulo 2) can be used to prove that $\sqrt{2}$ is irrational. The proof is by contradiction and first starts by assuming that this number is rational. Based on this assumption, it can be expressed in a *lowest terms fraction* as follows.

$$\sqrt{2} = \frac{p}{q} \tag{2.1}$$

Square both sides to obtain:

$$p^2 = 2 \cdot q^2 \tag{2.2}$$

Since the right hand side of the equation has a factor of 2, then p^2 must be even, which implies that p must be even. It therefore follows that:

$$\begin{aligned} & p = 2 \cdot k \\ & \Rightarrow 4 \cdot k^2 = 2 \cdot q^2 \\ & \Rightarrow 2 \cdot k^2 = q^2 \end{aligned} \tag{2.3}$$

This equation implies that q^2 is even and therefore requires q to be even. However, this is impossible because it was already shown that p must be even, and this would imply that there is no way to express $\sqrt{2}$ as a lowest terms fraction, or as any fraction for that matter. It therefore follows that the square root of 2 is irrational.

Modulo 3 Applications
Simple Way for Finding a Number Modulo 3

To find the remainder when any number is divided by 3, one can simply add up the digits and see the remainder for that number. For instance, 927652 **mod** 3 = 9+2+7+6+5+2 **mod** 3 = 32 **mod** 3 = 2. It is fairly simple to show why this rule is true. Consider any number, k. Let a_0 be the unit digit, a_1 be the tens digit a_2 be the 100's digit, and so on. This number can be written as:

$$k = a_0 + 10 \cdot a_1 + 100 \cdot a_2 + ... + 10^n \cdot a_n$$
$$= a_0 + a_1 + a_2 + ... + a_n + \left(9 \cdot a_1 + 99 \cdot a_2 + ... + (10^n - 1) \cdot a_n\right) \quad (2.4)$$

We see the term in parenthesis is divisible by 3, so this can be simplified using the modulus operator.

$$k \equiv a_0 + a_1 + a_2 + ... + a_n \ (\text{mod } 3) \quad (2.5)$$

So not only can this rule be used to find if a number is divisible by 3, but we see that the number modulo 3 is the same as the sum of the digits modulo 3.

Arithmetic Check

Because the remainder of a number is easy to calculate, this is a fast way to verify addition, subtraction, multiplication, and division for integers. Consider the following example:

$$534 \times 328 = 175252? \quad (2.6)$$

This math can be checked by taking both sides of the equation modulo 3.

$$534 \times 328 \equiv 175252? \ (\text{mod } 3)$$
$$(5+3+4) \times (3+2+8) \equiv (1+7+5+2+5+2)? \ (\text{mod } 3)$$
$$0 \times 1 \equiv 1? \ (\text{mod } 3) \quad \text{No!}$$

This simple check reveals that there is a mistake in this addition problem. This can be even simplified further. Consider the number 175252. When we do 1+7+5+2+5+2, we see that 7+5 = 12 and 2+5+2 = 9. Since these are both multiples of 3, we can cast them out to quickly get the correct remainder of 1.

Modulo 4 Application

Primitive Pythagorean Triples

Pythagorean Triples are positive integer solutions of the form (x, y, z) to the following equation:

$$x^2 + y^2 = z^2 \qquad (2.7)$$

Any solution to this equation can be multiplied by any positive integer to find another solution. For this reason, there is special interest in primitive Pythagorean triples of the form *(x, y, z)* for which all three of these numbers are relatively prime. Examples of these are as follows:

(3, 4, 5)	(5, 12, 13)	(8, 15, 17)	(7, 24, 25)
(20, 21, 29)	(12, 35, 37)	(9, 40, 41)	(28, 45, 53)
(11, 60, 61)	(16, 63, 65)	(33, 56, 65)	(48, 55, 73)
(13, 84, 85)	(36, 77, 85)	(39, 80, 89)	(65, 72, 97)

Note the following commonalities among the primitive Pythagorean triples:
- The largest one, z, is always odd
- Exactly one of x or y is divisible by 2
- Exactly one of x or y is divisible by 4
- Exactly one of x or y is divisible by 3
- Exactly one number is divisible by 5

All these properties can be proven with modular arithmetic. The last two properties can be proven with modulo 3 and 5 arithmetic, respectively. Modulo 4 arithmetic can be used to show that first three properties. To do this, consider the squares of various numbers modulo 4.

k mod 4	k^2 mod 4
0	0
1	1
2	0
3	1

***Table 2-3**   Squares in Modulo 4*

If z was even then z^2 ***mod 4*** would be zero, but that would force both x and y to be even, which cannot be the case since they are relatively prime. This establishes that z must be odd.

Because z is odd, then exactly one of x or y must be even. The reasoning behind this is if they were both odd, then this would imply that z is even, which is a contradiction. It therefore follows that exactly one of x or y is even. This establishes the first two properties.

To show the third property, one can make the simplifying assumption that *x* is odd and *y* is even. If it is the other way around, then switch the names and the following argument can still be used to show that exactly one of them is divisible by 4. The first step is to write the triple as follows.

$$(x, y, z) = (2 \cdot a + 1,\ 2 \cdot b,\ 2 \cdot c + 1) \tag{2.8}$$

Substituting this back into the original equation yields the following:

$$4 \cdot a^2 + 4 \cdot a + 1 + 4 \cdot b^2 = 4 \cdot c^2 + 4 \cdot c + 1 \tag{2.9}$$

Simplifying this yields:

$$b^2 = (c^2 + c) - (a^2 + a) \tag{2.10}$$

From this, we can reason that *b* is even because b^2 is the difference of two even quantities. Since *y* is twice *b*, this implies that *y* is divisible by 4. It therefore follows that exactly one of *x* or *y* is divisible by 4.

Modulo 6 Application

Prime Number Theorem

Prime numbers with the exception of 2 and 3 can be represented in the form $6 \cdot k \pm 1$, where **k** is a positive integer. This is easy to reason by considering any prime number, *P*, modulo 6. It cannot be 0, 2, 3, or 4, because otherwise it would be a multiple of 2 or 3. Therefore it follows that for any prime number that is not 2 or 3, ***P mod 6 = ± 1***.

Table 2-4 shows prime numbers generated with this method for values of **k** up to 20. Some values for **k** that do not have any prime numbers, while others have two. Notice that there are many primes that come in pairs that are two apart called *twin primes*. It turns out that there are infinitely many twin primes, but the proof of this is beyond the scope of this book.

k	$6 \cdot k \pm 1$	$6 \cdot k \pm 1$
1	5	7
2	11	13
3	17	19
4	23	~~25~~
5	29	31
6	~~35~~	37
7	41	43
8	47	~~49~~
9	53	~~55~~
10	59	61
11	~~65~~	67
12	71	73
13	~~77~~	79
14	83	~~85~~
15	89	~~91~~
16	~~95~~	97
17	101	103
18	107	109
19	113	~~115~~
20	~~119~~	~~121~~

Table 2-4   *Prime Number Table*

Modulo 7 Applications

Predicting the Day of the Week

As a result of the week being based on a 7 day cycle, modulo 7 arithmetic is very useful in relating the day of the week to the day of the month. By knowing that January 1, 2007 was a Monday and adding up all the months, days, and years since then, the day of the week can be calculated as follows:

$$Day\ of\ the\ week = \qquad (2.11)$$
$$[Day + MonthModulo + (Year - 2007) + $$
$$(LeapYearsSince\ 2007)\ ]\ mod\ 7$$

Day of the Week	Day Number
Sunday	0
Monday	1
Tuesday	2
Wednesday	3
Thursday	4
Friday	5
Saturday	6

Table 2-5   *Day Numbers*

For the month modulo number, one simply takes adds up all days before this month and takes this modulo 7. To speed up this calculation, Table 2-6 shows the modulo numbers for all months, but this might be hard to remember. If one just memorizes the numbers for January, April, July, and October, then one can easily find the other ones with minimal work. For instance, to get the modulo number for May, we know that it is one month after April which has Month Modulo of 6. So for May, we add 30 days for the previous month of April and we take 6+30 mod 7 to get one the month modulo number for May.

Month	Days	Month Modulo
January	31	0
February	28	3
March	31	3
April	30	6
May	31	1
June	30	4
July	31	6
August	31	2
September	30	5
October	31	0
November	30	3
December	31	5

Table 2-6 *Month Numbers*

For the years, because 365 is one greater than a multiple of 7, just add the years and add one more day for each leap year.

Example: Figure out the day of the week for October 27, 2010.

Day of Week = [27 + 0 + (2010–2007) + 1] mod 7 = [31] mod 7 = 3
So this day was a Wednesday.

Example: Figure out the day of the week May 17, 1970.

Day of Week = [17 + 1 + (1970 – 2007) +(– 9)] mod 7 = 0
So this day was a Sunday.

Example:
   Suppose you know that it is 2013 and it is a Wednesday in the month of September, but you cannot remember which day it is. It might be the 17th, or 18th, but you lost track of days and do not have a calendar handy. In this case, you know the day of the week, so the day can also be figured out.

$3 \equiv x + 5 + (2013 - 2007) + 2 \pmod{7} = 0$
$4 \equiv x \pmod{7}$

So it could be the 4th, 11th, 18th, or 25th, but since it is close to the 17th or 18th, the day is the 18th.

Modulo 9 Applications

Simple Way of Finding a Number Modulo 9

It is easy to prove that the remainder of the number modulo 9 is equal the remainder of the sum of the digits modulo 9. For any positive number, k, it can be expressed in this form:

$$k = a_0 + 10 \cdot a_1 + 100 \cdot a_2 + \ldots + 10^n \cdot a_n$$
$$= a_0 + a_1 + a_2 + \ldots + a_n + \left(9 \cdot a_1 + 99 \cdot a_2 + \ldots + (10^n - 1) \cdot a_n\right) \quad (2.12)$$

The term in parenthesis is divisible by 9, so this can be simplified using the modulus operator.

$$k \equiv a_0 + a_1 + a_2 + \ldots + a_n \pmod{9} \quad (2.13)$$

Arithmetic Checking with Modulo 9

One method for rapidly checking arithmetic problems involves modulo 9 arithmetic and is sometimes referred to as "casting out nines". The key concept is that the remainder of a number modulo 9 is the same as the sum of the digits modulo 9. For example, consider 485. $4 + 8 + 5 = 17$. 17 mod 9 = 8 = 485 mod 9. For faster results, sums of 9 can be cast out before the addition is performed. For example, with $4 + 8 + 5$, we see that the $4 + 5 = 9$, so the remainder is 8. For instance, suppose this was a multiple choice question:

    2347 × 1282 = ?
- a)   3088854
- b)   3008854
- c)   3253231
- d)   3173224

The first step is to take both the problem and the answers modulo 9.

2347 × 1282 ≡ 2347 (mod 9) × 1282 (mod 9) ≡ 7 × 4 ≡ 28 ≡ 1
- a)   3088854 (mod 9) ≡ 0
- b)   3008854 (mod 9) ≡ 1
- c)   3253231 (mod 9) ≡ 1
- d)   3173224 (mod 9) ≡ 5

We can see that either b) or c) could be the answer, but since we know that the result must be even, we can narrow this to the correct answer of b).

The same concept can be applied to addition and subtraction as well. Although the check can be fooled, it is a quick way to pick out careless errors in math calculations.

Modulo 11 Applications

Simple Way of Finding a Number Modulo 11

The remainder of a number modulo 11 is the difference of the sum of the even digits minus the sum of the odd digits. For instance, 235314 mod 11 = (2+5+1) − (3+3+4) mod 11 = 9. To prove this fact, let a_0 be the unit digit, a_1 be the tens digit a_2 be the 100's digit, and so on. This number can be written as:

$$k = a_0 + 10 \cdot a_1 + 100 \cdot a_2 + \ldots + 10^n \cdot a_n$$

$$= (a_0 + a_2 + \ldots + a_n) - (a_1 + a_3 + \ldots + a_{n-1}) \\ + \left\{ \begin{array}{l} [99 \cdot a_2 + 9999 \cdot a_4 \ldots + (10^n - 1) \cdot a_n] \\ + [11 \cdot a_1 + 1001 \cdot a_3 + (10^{n-1} + 1) \cdot a_{n-1}] \end{array} \right\} \quad (2.14)$$

Now consider the first term in the square brackets. Note that all the coefficients divisible by 11 and one less than some even power of 10. One can accept that this will always be divisible by 11, or this can be proven easily by mathematical induction. For the second term in brackets, notice that these terms are also all divisible by 11. This can also be easily be proven by mathematical induction. Therefore, if this equation is taken modulo 11, we get the desired result.

$$k \equiv (a_0 + a_2 + \ldots + a_n) - (a_1 + a_3 + \ldots + a_{n-1}) \pmod{11} \quad (2.15)$$

Arithmetic Check

Although the modulo 9 arithmetic check is more popular, the modulo 11 arithmetic check can also be used to check arithmetic and is harder to fool. An interesting application of this check is the validation of ISBN numbers on books. There are some weighting factors, but the basic check is modulo 11 to see if it is a valid number.

Modulo 12 Examples

The number 12 is commonly used in many systems because it is a relatively small number with a lot of factors. For example, Babylonians chose to base their number system on 12. Minutes, seconds, hours, and months are also based on multiples of 12. Another example is western music theory, which is the subject of the next chapter.

Other Applications of the Modulo Operator
Pseudo Random Number Generation

The generation of (pseudo) random numbers can be done by using a **modulus** (*M*) and a **seed** (x_0), and two prime numbers (P_1 and P_2). If the seed is picked in a somewhat random manner, then a sequence of random numbers can be calculated. Computers often use time as the seed value. Once one random number is known, the next number can be generated by the following equation.

$$x_{n+1} = x_n \cdot P_1 + P_2 \bmod M \qquad (2.16)$$

For instance to generate a sequence of random numbers between 0 and 100, one could use a seed of 0, modulus of 101, and prime numbers of 19 and 37 as shown in the following table.

n	$19 \cdot x_{n-1} + 37$	x[n]
0	–	0
1	37	37
2	740	33
3	664	58
4	1139	28
5	569	64
6	1253	41
7	816	8
8	189	88
9	1709	93
10	1804	87

Table 2-7 Pseudo Random Numbers

Proof that there are Infinitely Many Prime Numbers

Euclid's proof that there are infinitely many prime numbers uses the concept of remainder and is considered by many to be the most elegant proof in all of mathematics. The proof starts out by supposing that there are finitely many prime numbers and showing that this assumption leads to a contradiction. In other words, suppose that there were finitely many prime numbers with p_n being the largest one and consider the product of all of them.

$$2 \cdot 3 \cdot \ldots \cdot p_n + 1 \qquad (2.17)$$

This expression is a number (not infinite) and has a remainder of one when divided by any prime number. Because every whole number of 2 or greater is either prime or divisible by some prime and this number is neither, this is a contradiction. It therefore follows that the assumption that there were finitely many prime numbers was false and which proves that there are infinitely many prime numbers.

Chapter 3

Linear Modulus Equations of One Variable

Introduction

Modulus equations are those involving the modulus operator and can come up in many practical situations. This chapter introduces some basic properties and solution methods for linear modulus equations.

Properties of the Modulus Equations

Following are some theorems regarding the modulus operator that are fundamental for solving modular equations. For all these rules, X, Y, M, k, and n are assumed to be integers and it is also assumed that $M>0$. Some theorems are given nicknames so that they can easily be referenced, although these names are not necessarily standard names used in all textbooks.

Theorem 3.1   *Definition of Modulus*
If $x \equiv y \pmod{M}$ then $x = y + k \cdot M$

For example, if $x \equiv 5 \pmod{12}$ then $x = y + 12 \cdot k$. This rule proves to be especially useful in proving other theorems.

Theorem 3.2   *Addition/Subtraction Rule*
If $x \equiv y \pmod{M}$ then $x \pm a \equiv y \pm a \pmod{M}$

This rule states that an equal value can be added or subtracted from both sides of a modular equation. For example, if $x + 5 \equiv 3 \pmod{7}$ then $x \equiv -2 \equiv 5 \pmod{7}$.

Theorem 3.3   *Reduction of Modulus*
If $x \equiv y \pmod{n \cdot M}$ then $x \equiv y \pmod{M}$.

This theorem is useful in proving other theorems and reducing equations. Be aware that applying this rule can create extraneous solutions to an equation. For example, $x \equiv 5 \pmod{12}$ implies that $x \equiv 5 \pmod{4}$. Although it is true that 5 is a solution to the original equation, the reduction of modulus has also created the extraneous solution of 9.

Theorem 3.4   Division/Multiplication Rule

$n \cdot X \equiv n \cdot Y \pmod{M}$ and $X \equiv Y \left(mod \ \dfrac{M}{GCD(n,M)} \right)$ are equivalent.

This theorem shows that division can be done with modulus equations, but if the divisor shares any common factor with the modulus, then the modulus is reduced by this factor. This rule can also be reversed and used as multiplication rule. Below are several examples how this rule can be applied.

$$\begin{aligned} 7 \cdot x &\equiv 21 \pmod{30} &\Leftrightarrow & \quad x \equiv 3 \pmod{30} \\ 6 \cdot x &\equiv 12 \pmod{15} &\Leftrightarrow & \quad x \equiv 2 \pmod{5} \\ \tfrac{1}{6} \cdot x &\equiv 3 \pmod{15} &\Leftrightarrow & \quad x \equiv 18 \pmod{45} \\ -x &\equiv 3 \pmod{7} &\Leftrightarrow & \quad x \equiv -3 \pmod{7} \end{aligned} \qquad (3.1)$$

Solving the Linear Equation of One Variable

Linear equations such as (3.2) do not always have a solution, but there is a definitive test to know. Theorem 3.5 discusses the necessary conditions for the existence and uniqueness of a solution

$$a \cdot x \equiv b \pmod{M} \qquad (3.2)$$

Theorem 3.5   Linear Equation Solution and Existence

Consider the equation $a \cdot x \equiv b \pmod{M}$ where a is not equivalent to zero. A solution exists and is unique modulo $M/GCD(a,b)$ if and only if:

$$b \ mod \ GCD(a,M) \equiv 0 \qquad (3.3)$$

Putting this theorem in other words, if a has a common factor with M, then it must also be common to b. In order to solve the equation when there is a solution, one can divide through by the common factor of $GCD(a, M)$. The following examples show how to apply this theorem.

Example: Solve $2 \cdot x \equiv 4 \pmod{7}$
Solution:
Divide through by 2 to get the solution of $x \equiv 2 \pmod{7}$

Example: Solve $12 \cdot x \equiv 14 \pmod{40}$
Solution:
Because 4 is common to 12 and 40, but not 14, no solution exists.

When the equation $a \cdot x \equiv b \pmod{M}$ has been shown to have a solution, it might not be obvious how to divide b by a as shown in the following example.

$$3 \cdot x \equiv 7 \pmod{11} \tag{3.4}$$

One approach to solve this equation is to add 11 to both sides of the equation so that the right hand side can be expressed in a form that is more obviously divisible by 3. The left hand side is unchanged by adding this factor of 11.

$$\begin{aligned} 3 \cdot x &\equiv 18 \pmod{11} \\ x &\equiv 6 \pmod{11} \end{aligned} \tag{3.5}$$

An alternative approach to solving (3.4) is to multiply both sides of the equation by 4 as shown below.

$$\begin{aligned} 12 \cdot x &\equiv 28 \pmod{11} \\ x &\equiv 6 \pmod{11} \end{aligned} \tag{3.6}$$

Both methods worked for solving equation (3.4), but a more systematic method is necessary for figuring out what value to add or multiply by when it is not obvious.

Solution Method by Addition

This method of solution involves adding a multiple of the modulus the right of the equation, which allows it to be expressed in an equivalent form that makes the division obvious. To solve the equation (3.2), first try to add some multiple of M to the right hand side that makes both sides divisible by a.

$$\begin{aligned} a \cdot x &\equiv b + k_1 \cdot M \pmod{M} \\ b + k_1 \cdot M &\equiv 0 \pmod{a} \\ k_1 \cdot M &\equiv -b \pmod{a} \end{aligned} \tag{3.7}$$

If (3.7) is too difficult to solve, another equation can be set up to solve for k_1.

$$\begin{aligned} -b + k_2 \cdot a &\equiv 0 \pmod{k_1} \\ k_2 \cdot a &\equiv b \pmod{k_1} \end{aligned} \tag{3.8}$$

If (3.8) is still too difficult to solve, then this technique can be continued further.

$$\begin{aligned} b + k_3 \cdot k_1 &\equiv 0 \pmod{k_2} \\ k_3 \cdot k_1 &\equiv -b \pmod{k_2} \end{aligned} \tag{3.9}$$

Every time this process is continued, the numbers involved get smaller until eventually the last value of k_n can be found and then used to solve all the equations leading to it. Throughout this process, substantial simplifications can be made by eliminating multiples of the modulus from the known quantities.

Example:
Solve the following equation.

$$7 \cdot x \equiv 11 \pmod{29} \tag{3.10}$$

Solution:
Set up a series of equations to figure out what multiple of the modulus to add.

$$\begin{aligned} 7 \cdot x &\equiv 11 + 29 \cdot k_1 \pmod{29} \\ 11 + 29 \cdot k_1 &\equiv 0 \pmod{7} \\ 4 + 1 \cdot k_1 &\equiv 0 \pmod{7} \\ k_1 &\equiv 3 \pmod{7} \end{aligned} \tag{3.11}$$

Now substitute this backwards to find the solution.

$$\begin{aligned} 7 \cdot x &\equiv 11 + 29 \cdot (3) \pmod{29} \\ 7 \cdot x &\equiv 98 \pmod{29} \\ x &\equiv 14 \pmod{29} \end{aligned} \tag{3.12}$$

Example:
Solve the following equation.

$$2205 \cdot x \equiv 4991 \pmod{7189} \tag{3.13}$$

Solution:
The first step is to divide through by the common factor of 7.

$$315 \cdot x \equiv 713 \pmod{1027} \tag{3.14}$$

Table 3-3 summarizes the other solution steps to solving this.

Forward	Back Substitution
$315 \cdot x \equiv 713 + 1027 \cdot k_1 \pmod{1027}$	$315 \cdot x \equiv 713 + 1027 \cdot 241 \pmod{1027}$ $x \equiv 788 \pmod{1027}$
$713 + 1027 \cdot k_1 \equiv 0 \pmod{315}$ $82 \cdot k_1 \equiv -83 \pmod{315}$	$82 \cdot k_1 \equiv -83 + 315 \cdot 63 \pmod{315}$ $k_1 \equiv 241 \pmod{315}$
$-83 + 315 \cdot k_2 \equiv 0 \pmod{82}$ $69 \cdot k_2 \equiv 1 \pmod{82}$	$69 \cdot k_2 \equiv 1 + 82 \cdot 53 \pmod{82}$ $k_2 \equiv 63 \pmod{82}$
$1 + 82 \cdot k_3 \equiv 0 \pmod{69}$ $13 \cdot k_3 \equiv -1 \pmod{69}$	$13 \cdot k_3 \equiv -1 + 10 \cdot 69 \pmod{69}$ $k_3 \equiv 53 \pmod{69}$
$-1 + 69 \cdot k_4 \equiv 0 \pmod{13}$ $4 \cdot k_4 \equiv 1 \pmod{13}$	$4 \cdot k_4 \equiv 1 + 13 \cdot 3 \pmod{13}$ $k_4 \equiv 10 \pmod{13}$
$1 + 13 \cdot k_5 \equiv 0 \pmod{4}$ $1 \cdot k_5 \equiv 3 \pmod{4}$	$k_5 \equiv 3 \pmod{4}$

Table 3-3   *Solution Method Example*

Solution Method by Multiplication - Inverses in Modular Arithmetic

The equation (3.2) can also be solved by multiplying both sides by the inverse of *a*, which typically written as a^{-1}. To find the inverse of *a* mod *M*, this can be found by solving the following equation.

$$a \cdot x \equiv 1 \pmod{M} \qquad (3.15)$$

For example, to find the inverse of 5 modulo 7, we solve $5 \cdot x \equiv 1 \pmod 7$, which has the solution of $x \equiv 3 \pmod 7$. A consequence of (3.15) and the Linear Equation Theorem is that the inverse of a number, *a*, exists if and only if *a* and *M* are relatively prime. Finding the inverse by hand can be just as much effort as solving the equation using the addition method that was already discussed. However, the advantages of using the inverse method to solve (3.2) are that it can be used if *b* is left as an unknown and that a table of modular inverses can be computed, such as Table 3-4. The table only goes up to half the modulus because the following rule can be used to easily find the other half.

$$(-a)^{-1} \equiv -a^{-1} \pmod{M} \qquad (3.16)$$

For instance, inverse of 26 modulo 49 is not directly shown on the table. To find this inverse, instead find the inverse of $-26 \equiv 23$, which can be computed from the table as 32. Since this is the negative of what we really wanted, we realize that –32 is equivalent to 17 modulo 49, so this inverse is 17.

	Number																							
Modulus	2	3	4	5	6	7	8	9	10	11	12	13	14	15	16	17	18	19	20	21	22	23	24	25
3	2																							
4	X	3																						
5	3	2	4																					
6	X	X	X	5																				
7	4	5	2	3	6																			
8	X	3	X	5	X	7																		
9	5	X	7	2	X	4	8																	
10	X	7	X	X	X	3	X	9																
11	6	4	3	9	2	8	7	5	10															
12	X	X	X	5	X	7	X	X	X	11														
13	7	9	10	8	11	2	5	3	4	6	12													
14	X	5	X	3	X	X	X	11	X	9	X	13												
15	8	X	4	X	X	13	2	X	X	11	X	7	14											
16	X	11	X	13	X	7	X	9	X	3	X	5	X	15										
17	9	6	13	7	3	5	15	2	12	14	10	4	11	8	16									
18	X	X	X	11	X	13	X	X	X	5	X	7	X	X	X	17								
19	10	13	5	4	16	11	12	17	2	7	8	3	15	14	6	9	18							
20	X	7	X	X	X	3	X	9	X	11	X	17	X	X	X	13	X	19						
21	11	X	16	17	X	X	8	X	19	2	X	13	X	X	4	5	X	10	20					
22	X	15	X	9	X	19	X	5	X	X	X	17	X	3	X	13	X	7	X	21				
23	12	8	6	14	4	10	3	18	7	21	2	16	5	20	13	19	9	17	15	11	22			
24	X	X	X	5	X	7	X	X	X	11	X	13	X	X	X	17	X	19	X	X	X	23		
25	13	17	19	X	21	18	22	14	X	16	23	2	9	X	11	3	7	4	X	6	8	12	24	
26	X	9	X	21	X	15	X	3	X	19	X	X	X	7	X	23	X	11	X	5	X	17	X	25
27	14	X	7	11	X	4	17	X	19	5	X	25	2	X	22	8	X	10	23	X	16	20	X	13
28	X	19	X	17	X	X	X	25	X	23	X	13	X	15	X	5	X	3	X	X	X	11	X	9
29	15	10	22	6	5	25	11	13	3	8	17	9	27	2	20	12	21	26	16	18	4	24	23	7
30	X	X	X	X	X	13	X	X	X	11	X	7	X	X	X	23	X	19	X	X	X	17	X	X
31	16	21	8	25	26	9	4	7	28	17	13	12	20	29	2	11	19	18	14	3	24	27	22	5
32	X	11	X	13	X	23	X	25	X	3	X	5	X	15	X	17	X	27	X	29	X	7	X	9
33	17	X	25	20	X	19	29	X	10	3	X	28	26	X	31	2	X	7	5	X	X	23	X	4
34	X	23	X	7	X	5	X	19	X	31	X	21	X	25	X	X	X	9	X	13	X	3	X	15
35	18	12	9	X	6	X	22	4	X	16	3	27	X	X	11	33	2	24	X	X	8	32	19	X
36	X	X	X	29	X	31	X	X	X	23	X	25	X	X	X	17	X	19	X	X	X	11	X	13
37	19	25	28	15	31	16	14	33	26	27	34	20	8	5	7	24	35	2	13	30	32	29	17	3
38	X	13	X	23	X	11	X	17	X	7	X	X	X	33	X	9	X	X	X	29	X	5	X	35
39	20	X	10	8	X	28	5	X	4	32	X	X	14	X	22	23	X	37	2	X	16	17	X	25
40	X	27	X	X	X	23	X	9	X	11	X	37	X	X	X	33	X	19	X	21	X	7	X	X
41	21	14	31	33	7	6	36	32	37	15	24	19	3	11	18	29	16	13	39	2	28	25	12	23
42	X	X	X	17	X	X	X	X	X	23	X	13	X	X	X	5	X	31	X	X	X	11	X	37
43	22	29	11	26	36	37	27	24	13	4	18	10	40	23	35	38	12	34	28	41	2	15	9	31
44	X	15	X	9	X	19	X	5	X	X	X	17	X	3	X	13	X	7	X	21	X	23	X	37
45	23	X	34	X	X	13	17	X	X	41	X	7	X	29	X	31	8	X	19	X	X	43	2	X
46	X	31	X	37	X	33	X	41	X	21	X	39	X	43	X	19	X	17	X	11	X	X	X	35
47	24	16	12	19	8	27	6	21	33	30	4	29	37	22	3	36	34	5	40	9	15	45	2	32
48	X	X	X	29	X	7	X	X	X	35	X	37	X	X	X	17	X	43	X	X	X	23	X	25
49	25	33	37	10	41	X	43	11	5	9	45	34	X	36	46	26	30	31	27	X	29	32	47	2
50	X	17	X	X	X	43	X	39	X	41	X	27	X	X	X	3	X	29	X	31	X	37	X	X

Table 3-4   *Modular Inverses Up to 50*

As an example of how use this table, consider the equation $7 \cdot x \equiv 4 \ (mod \ 15)$. To solve this, look up the inverse of 7 modulo 15, which is 13. Then multiply both sides of the equation by 13 to get $13 \cdot 7 \cdot x \equiv 4 \cdot 13 \ (mod \ 15)$, which simplifies to $x \equiv 7 \ (mod \ 15)$. In Table 3-4, note that inverse of a number exists and is unique if and only if it has no common factors with the modulus.

Modular inverses also allow one to define fractions in modular arithmetic. For instance, the inverse of 5 modulo 7 is 3, or in other words, the following is true:

$$\frac{1}{5} \equiv 3 \ (mod \ 7) \tag{3.17}$$

Because not all inverses exist, it follows that not all fractions will be defined. Nevertheless, when dealing with expressions and equations, it is sometimes easier to do all the combining and simplification of terms using regular (non-modular) arithmetic and then convert all fractions back to whole numbers in modular arithmetic as a final step.

Systems of Linear Equations

In order to solve a system of equations, the general method is to find an expression from the first equation, and then substitute this into the next expression and continue this process until a solution is found. However, there is an elegant result called the Chinese Remainder Theorem that specifies the conditions for which a solution exists.

Theorem 3.6   Chinese Remainder Theorem

Consider the following system of equations:

$$x \equiv a_1 \pmod{M_1}$$
$$x \equiv a_2 \pmod{M_2}$$
$$\ldots \tag{3.18}$$
$$x \equiv a_n \pmod{M_n}$$

This system has a solution if and only if

$$a_1 \equiv a_2 \equiv \ldots \equiv a_n \,(\bmod\ GCD(M_1, M_2, \ldots, M_n)) \tag{3.19}$$

Furthermore the solution is unique modulo

$$LCM(M_1, M_2, \ldots, M_n) \tag{3.20}$$

Proof
The proof of this is left to reference [1].

Given that a solution exists, the general solution method is to assume a solution of the form:

$$x = a_1 + k_1 \cdot M_1 \tag{3.21}$$

This will satisfy the first of the solution of equations (3.18). The next step is to substitute this into the second equation of the solution of equations (3.18) to find an equation for k_2. This process continues until a solution is found.

Example
Solve the following system of equations:

$$x \equiv 7 \ (\text{Mod } 15)$$
$$x \equiv 10 \ (\text{Mod } 21) \quad (3.22)$$
$$x \equiv 4 \ (\text{Mod } 51)$$

The first step is to see if a solution exists by first calculating the greatest common divisor and making sure that all the coefficients are equivalent by this modulus, which is the case.

$$GCD(15, 21, 51) = 3$$
$$7 \bmod 3 = 1$$
$$4 \bmod 3 = 1 \quad (3.23)$$
$$10 \bmod 3 = 1$$

The next step is to calculate the least common multiple to know by what modulus the solution is unique by.

$$LCM(15, 21, 51) = 1785 \quad (3.24)$$

The first equation implies a solution of the form:

$$x = 7 + k_1 \cdot 15 \quad (3.25)$$

Substituting this into the second equation yields more information on k_1.

$$7 + k_1 \cdot 15 \equiv 10 \ (\text{mod } 21)$$
$$15 \cdot k_1 \equiv 3 \equiv 45 \ (\text{mod } 21)$$
$$\Rightarrow k_1 \equiv 3 \ (\text{mod } 7) \quad (3.26)$$
$$\Rightarrow k_1 = 3 + 7 \cdot k_2$$

This value of k_1 can be used to calculate x and used into the third equation.

$$7 + (3 + 7 \cdot k_2) \cdot 15 \equiv 4 \ (\text{mod } 51)$$
$$3 \cdot k_2 \equiv 3 \ (\text{mod } 51) \quad (3.27)$$
$$k_2 = 1$$

Substituting this result into and (3.26) to get k_1 and then this result into (3.25) yields the solution.

$$k_1 = 3 + 7 \cdot 1 = 10$$
$$x = 7 + 10 \cdot 15 = 157 \quad (3.28)$$

So the solution is 157, which is unique modulo 1785. This particular example is motivated by a radar application mentioned in reference [2]. The general idea of radar is to send out periodic waveforms and then see how long it takes for the signal to return in order to calculate the distance the object away. Because the waveform is periodic, we need to know which cycle of the received radar was received. By combining multiple radar waveforms, the range can be increased. The advantage to doing it this way, as opposed to doing it in a single radar waveform with a longer period is that it has a steeper slope with less sensitivity to noise or interference.

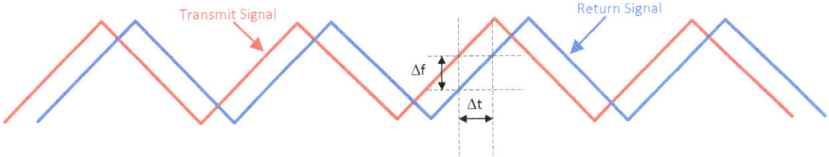

Figure 3-1   *Typical Radar Ramping Signal*

References
[1]   Fergusen, Kevin *"Chinese Remainder Theorem Proof"*. Retrieved October 28, 2013 from http://planetmath.org/encyclopedia/ChineseRemainderTheoremProof.htm.

[2]   http://mathoverflow.net/questions/10014/applications-of-the-chinese-remainder-theorem   Retrieved October 28, 2013

Appendix: Proof of Various Rules

Theorem 3.3   Reduction of Modulus Rule
If $X \equiv Y \pmod{n \cdot M}$ then $X \equiv Y \pmod{M}$.

Proof
To prove this theorem, reason that if $X \equiv Y \pmod{n \cdot M}$, then the definition of modulus implies that $X = Y + k \cdot M$, where k can be any integer. Take both sides of this equation modulo M to get $X \equiv Y \pmod{M}$, which is the desired result.

Theorem 3.4   Division/Multiplication Rule
The conditions $n \cdot X \equiv n \cdot Y \pmod{M}$ and $X \equiv Y \pmod{M / GCD(M, n)}$ are equivalent.

Proof
Part 1:
First assume that $n \cdot X \equiv n \cdot Y \pmod{M}$ and express this relationship as:

$$n \cdot X \equiv n \cdot Y \left(mod \left(GCD(M,n) \cdot \frac{M}{GCD(M,n)} \right) \right) \qquad (3.29)$$

Then use the reduction of modulus theorem to reduce the modulus.

$$n \cdot X \equiv n \cdot Y \left(mod \left(\frac{M}{GCD(M,n)} \right) \right) \qquad (3.30)$$

By the definition of modulus, this can be written in the following form.

$$n \cdot X - n \cdot Y = k \cdot \frac{M}{GCD(M,n)} \qquad (3.31)$$

Now n cannot divide $\frac{M}{GCD(M,n)}$ because this would imply that the $GCD(M,n)$ could be a factor of n larger, which contradictions the definition of it being the *greatest* common divisor. Therefore, n must divide k and one can divide the equation through by n to get the desired result.

Part 2:
The second step is to prove that (3.32) implies $n \cdot X \equiv n \cdot Y \pmod{M}$.

$$X \equiv Y \left(mod \ \frac{M}{GCD(M,n)} \right) \qquad (3.32)$$

Equation (3.33) can be obtained by applying the definition of modulus and multiplying through by **n**. This result can be taken modulo **M** in order to prove the theorem.

$$n \cdot X - n \cdot Y \equiv \left(\frac{n}{GCD(M,n)} \right) \cdot M \qquad (3.33)$$

Theorem 3.5 *Linear Equation Existence and Uniqueness*

Consider the equation $a \cdot x \equiv b \pmod{M}$ where **a** is not equivalent to zero. A solution exists and it is unique modulo $M/GCD(a,b)$ if and only if:

$$b \ mod \ GCD(a,M) \equiv 0 \qquad (3.34)$$

Proof:
By realizing that $GCD(a, M)$ divides both **a** and **M** and applying the reduction of modulus theorem, this establishes that (3.34) is a necessary condition for a solution to exist.

To show that (3.34) is a sufficient condition for a solution to exist, divide through the linear equation by $GCD(a,M)$ which we know will divide **a**, **b**, and **M**) and apply the division rule to obtain the following result.

$$\frac{a}{GCD(a,M)} \cdot x \equiv \frac{b}{GCD(a,M)} \left(mod \ \frac{M}{GCD(a,M)} \right) \qquad (3.35)$$

Define some new variables, **a***, **b***, and **M*** and rewrite (3.35) as follows:

$$a^* \cdot x \equiv b^* \pmod{M^*} \qquad (3.36)$$

a* and **M*** will have no common factors because the greatest common factor has been divided out. Define the function $f(x) = a^* \cdot x$ and realize $f(x) \equiv f(y) \pmod{M^*}$ implies that $x \equiv y \pmod{M^*}$, because the division rule can be applied with the knowledge that **a*** and **M*** have no common factors, thus implying that *f(x)* is a one-to-one function. Now there are **M*** possible values that **x** can assume and also exactly **M*** possible values that **b*** can assume. This implies that one of the possible value values for **x** must satisfy the equation $a^* \cdot x \equiv b \pmod{M^*}$, which establishes that a solution exists.

Chapter 4

Integer Arithmetic Applications to Music Theory

Introduction

Music theory is an excellent example of discrete principles applied to a continuous application. Although it is possible to produce a continuous range of frequencies, music is defined as having these frequencies confined to discrete values in order to make it sound better. For instance, the frequency of the note on the violin is controlled by which string is being played and the position of the finger on that string. Although it is possible to put the finger in any position, the fingers are placed in specific discrete positions, not just anywhere. The piano is an excellent tool for understanding the discrete notes of music theory because it gives a visual and sound representation of all the notes.

Music has an elegant mathematical foundation based on twelve notes that are evenly spaced apart, but this even spacing of notes is not clear from the way that the notes are named and written on lines of music. Once one untangles the definitions used in music, then the patterns, intentions, and elegance of music theory become clear.

Theory of Musical Notes

The mathematics of western music theory is based on a factor of two in frequency, which is defined as an *octave*. The octave is then divided into twelve musical notes which are the same multiple apart. To get from one note to the next, one multiplies the frequency of by $2^{(1/12)} \sim 1.059$, which is called a *half step*. The half step technically refers to multiplying the frequency by a constant instead of adding a constant to the frequency, but one could simply think in terms of $10 \cdot log|Frequency|$, which would then the half step equivalent to a 0.25 dB frequency change. The concepts of harmonies, chords, scales, and key signatures are all implied by the key fact that the notes are separated by a half step.

It would make the most mathematical sense to start off with note 0 and end with note 11 as shown in Table 4-3. However, music defines the notes differently as seven fundamental notes of A, B, C, D, E, F, and G with the ability to shift up a half step by making it *sharp* (♯) or down a half step by making it *flat* (♭). Going up one half step or going down a half step from the next higher note lead to the frequency. In other words, C♯ and D♭ are the same note. Note that there is only a half step between B and C and also between E and F, which means that there is no such thing as B#, because this would be C. Music also defines the *whole step* as two half steps, which is a multiple of $2^{(2/12)} \sim 1.122$.

Note Number	Musical Note	Possible Frequency (Hz)
0	A	440.0000
1	A♯ and B♭	466.1638
2	B	493.8833
3	C	523.2511
4	C♯ and D♭	554.3653
5	D	587.3295
6	D♯ and E♭	622.2540
7	E	659.2551
8	F	698.4565
9	F♯ and G♭	739.9888
10	G	783.9909
11	G♯ and A♭	830.6094
12	A (next octave higher)	880.0000

Table 4-3   Frequencies of Musical Notes

The *A* note in this table is an even 440 Hz, which the note that the concertmaster violinist plays for the rest of the orchestra to tune the other instruments. There are other versions of *A* that are powers of two off such as 110 Hz, 220 Hz, 880 Hz, and many others. Although these frequencies are different, playing a lower frequency version of the *A* note will also produce some of the higher frequency multiple versions of the *A*, so they have the same letter name and share many of the ways that they resonate with other notes, but their sound is different. From a notation point of view, we might say that notes 5 and 17 are both the note *D*, but use the note 17 to denote the higher octave.

Even though the note *A* is theoretically the only rational frequency, the trained musical ear might only be able to tell to the closest one or two Hz, so practically we can think of these note frequencies rounded to the nearest Hz or so.

Intervals and the Theory Musical Harmony of Two Notes

The spacing between two notes is called the *musical interval*. This is expressed in half steps and what determines if these two notes will sound well together. If the interval has a *frequency ratio* that looks like a simple fraction and is reasonably close, then the human ear will interpret it as such and the two notes will sound harmonious together.

Half Steps	Frequency Ratio	Approximate Frequency Ratio	Approximation Error	Common Musical Name
0	1.000	1	0.0%	Unison
1	1.059			Minor Second
2	1.122	9/8	0.2%	Second
3	1.189	6/5	0.9%	Minor Third
4	1.260	5/4	−0.8%	Third
5	1.335	4/3	−0.1%	Fourth
6	1.414	7/5	−1.0%	Minor Fifth
7	1.498	3/2	0.1%	Fifth
8	1.587	8/5	0.8%	Minor Sixth
9	1.682	5/3	−0.9%	Sixth
10	1.782	7/4	1.0%	Minor Seventh
11	1.888	9/5	−0.7%	Seventh
12	2.000	2	0.0%	Octave

Table 4-4   *Frequencies of Musical Notes*

Table 4-4 shows frequency ratios and their common musical names. To get the frequency ratio from the relative frequency, just round it to the closest fraction, because this is more like the human ear will perceive these frequencies. One may wonder where the common musical names come from, especially the *octave* which is a factor of two in frequency, not eight. To get the musical name, one starts with the *A* note and counts up the number of half steps to the final note and then each whole letter in the sequence. For instance, a *fifth* is seven half steps which would look as follows:

$$A \rightarrow A\# \rightarrow B \rightarrow C \rightarrow C\# \rightarrow D \rightarrow D\# \rightarrow E$$

The problem with the musical names is that if one starts at something other than the *A* note, this rule does not always work. For this reason, it may be easier to think of these musical names in terms of how many half steps they are, because this is independent of the starting note.

Two notes will sound well when played together if the ratio of their frequencies is close to simple fraction. For instance, if one frequency is twice the frequency of the other, then their combination will have a nice periodic waveform as shown in Figure 4-1. The ear can sense that these frequencies are nicely related and they will sound harmonious together.

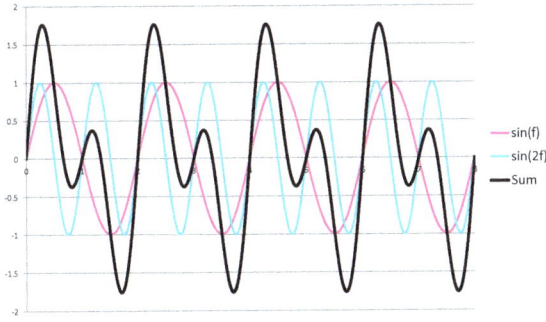

Figure 4-1   *A Perfect Octave*

Contrast this with two notes that are not nicely related as shown in Figure 4-2.

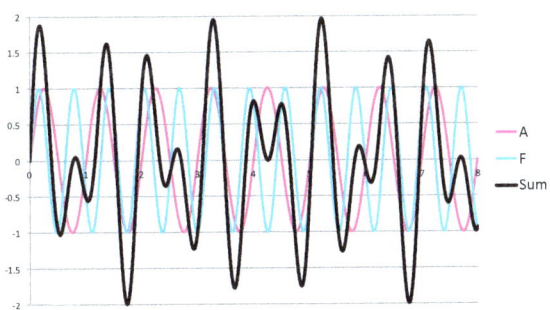

Figure 4-2   *Nonharmonious 8 Half Steps Apart*

After the octave, the next harmonious combination would be the fifth, which has a frequency ratio that is very close to 3/2. The fifth is fundamental to music theory and many instruments are based on it, such as the strings on the violin.

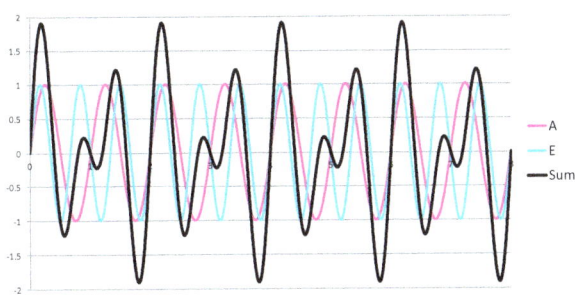

Figure 4-3   *A Perfect Fifth*

Figure 4-3 shows a fifth and demonstrates that the sum has twice the period and therefore half the frequency of the lowest frequency A note. If the A and E notes were different phases or amplitudes, the sum might have a different looking waveform, but the period and frequency would be the same. The higher the frequency of this sum relative to the lowest frequency note, the more harmonious the notes sound together. To express this mathematically, if we consider the relative frequency of the lowest note to be one and the frequency of the higher note in this case would be 3/2 times that, then GCD(1, 3/2) = ½, which is fairly large compared to many other two note combinations.

After the octave and the fifth, the next most harmonious combination of two notes would be the *fourth*, which has a spacing of five half steps with a fraction of 4/3. When these two notes are played together, the frequency of their combination would be GCD(1, 4/3) = 1/3 of the lowest frequency note. Following this there is the *third* with a frequency ratio of 5/4 and a spacing of 4 half steps. For the third, we can calculate the relative frequency of the combination as GCD(1, 5/4) = ¼. Following the third is the *minor third*, which has a frequency ratio of 6/5, a spacing of 3 half steps, and where the combination of the two notes has a frequency of GCD(1, 6/5) = 1/5 of the lowest frequency note. There are other combinations as well, but they become less harmonious. Not only is this GCD frequency lower, but also the frequency ratios are more approximate and more rounded off than they are for the octave, fifth, fourth, third, and minor third.

Chords and the Theory of Musical Harmony

When three or more harmonious notes are played simultaneously is called a *chord*. The most harmonious three note chord would be to play the same note in three different octaves, like 0, 12, and 24. This will resonate well together, but there are other possibilities as well. If a fifth and an octave is played together, then the relative frequency of this combination will be GCD(1, 3/2, 2) = ½. These combinations of notes do sound well together, but perhaps they are too obvious to be given special names.

The next most harmonious combination would be the *major chord*, which is a combination of a third and a fifth. For this we calculate GCD(1, 5/4, 3/2) = ¼. This implies that the period of the combination of these notes is four times the period of the fundamental, which is apparent in Figure 4-4.

Note Spacing	Ratio	Step Name
0	1	Fundamental
4	5/4	Third
7	3/2	Fifth

Table 4-5   *Notes for a Major Chord*

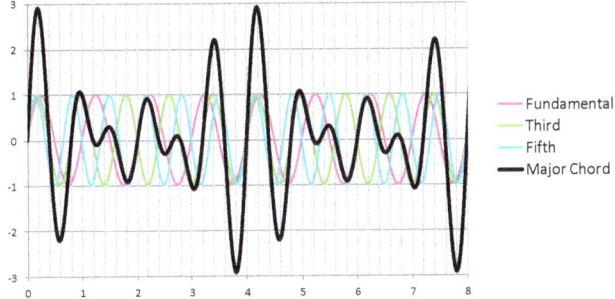

Figure 4-4   *Two Periods of a Major Chord*

There are several variations that are possible with the major chord. For instance, one can add in another note with spacing of 12 to make a perfect octave. Similar harmonies based on this are possible by shifting any of the notes up or down an octave, which is equivalent to adding or subtracting 12 half steps. Some variations of this major chord could be the notes 0, 16, and 7 or 0, 4, and 19.

The *minor chord* is a combination of a *minor third* and a fifth, which would be , for which the combination has a relative frequency of GCD(1, 6/5, 3/2) = 1/10.

Half Steps	Close Fraction	Name
0	1	Unison
3	6/5	Minor Third
7	3/2	Fifth

Table 4-6   *Notes for a Minor Chord*

As Figure 4-5 shows, the period of the minor chord is ten times that of the fundamental. This combination does sound well together, but sounds less together than the major chord and is more often used in music with more sad tones.

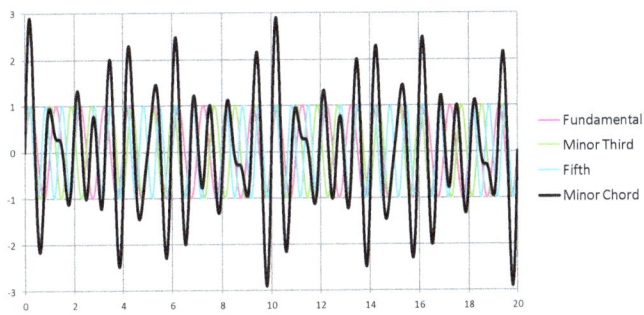

Figure 4-5   *Two Periods of a Minor Chord*

Scales and Key Signatures

Aside from playing notes simultaneously together to make chords, they can also be played in succession as well. A *scale* is a collection of notes in ascending order that are played in sequence. Scales typically have seven notes per octave and the first and last notes of the scale are the same letter name, although it is one or more octaves higher or lower. Typically scales are named by the note that they start with.

Many songs can be formed by choosing just the notes from a particular scale. There are accommodations to add sharps and flats manually if there is some note that really needs to be added, but this is not necessary in many cases. The scale on which a musical piece is created is called the *key signature*.

Major Scales and Key Signatures

Table 4-7, shows a *major scale* that contains a major chord and several other notes to fill in the gaps. It can be thought of as steps of whole, whole, half, whole, whole, whole, half as shown in Table 4-3.

Half Steps	Frequency Ratio	Common Musical Name	Step from Last Note
0	1	Fundamental	n/a
2	7/8	Second	Whole
4	5/4	Third	Whole
5	4/3	Fourth	Half
7	3/2	Fifth	Whole
9	5/3	Sixth	Whole
11	9/5	Seventh	Whole
12	2	Octave	Half

Table 4-7   Major Scale

If one starts out with the C note and applies these intervals, this will form a C major scale with the notes of C,D,E,F,G,A,B, C. The C major has no sharps or flats and has a sequence of 3,5,7,8,10,12,14, and 15. For all other major scales, there will be at least one sharp or flat. Typically these are memorized, but these elegant formulas summarize the relationship.

$$MajorKey \equiv 7 \times Sharps + 3 \ (mod \ 12) \qquad (4.1)$$

$$MajorKey \equiv -7 \times Flats + 3 \ (mod \ 12) \qquad (4.2)$$

For instance, if there are 5 sharps, this key would be the note name of 38 *mod* 12 = 2, which is the key of **B**. If there were 4 flats, this would be the key of –25 mod 12 = 11, which would be the key of *A* ♭ (which is the same as *G*♯). By multiplying both sides of equation (4.1) by 7 and both sides of equation (4.2) by –7, one can also derive the relationships that say how many sharps or flats a given key signature has. Note that a key will have only sharps or flats, typically whichever is least. For instance, the key of *A* major is said to have 3 sharps, not 9 flats.

$$Sharps \equiv 7 \times MajorKey + 3 \ (mod \ 12) \qquad (4.3)$$

$$Flats \equiv -7 \times MajorKey - 3 \ (mod \ 12) \qquad (4.4)$$

Minor Scales and Key Signatures

The pattern for the *minor scale* is whole step, half step, whole step, whole step, half step whole step, whole step as shown in Table 4-8.

Half Steps	Frequency Ratio	Common Musical Name	Step from Last Note
0	1	Fundamental	n/a
2	9/8	Minor Second	Whole
3	6/5	Minor Third	Half
5	4/3	Fourth	Whole
7	3/2	Fifth	Whole
8	5/3	Minor Sixth	Half
10	7/4	Minor Seventh	Whole
12	2	Octave	Whole

Table 4-8 *Minor Scale Intervals*

For minor keys, A minor is the key that has no sharps or flats. The formulas for the minor keys are as follows:

$$MinorKey \equiv 7 \times Sharps \ (mod \ 12) \qquad (4.5)$$

$$MinorKey \equiv -7 \times Flats \ (mod \ 12) \qquad (4.6)$$

For instance, if there are 5 sharps, this key would be the note name of 35 mod 12 = 11, which is the key of G♯ minor. If there were 4 flats, this would be the key of –28 mod 12 = 8, which would be the key of F minor. By multiplying both sides of equation (4.5) by 7 and both sides of equation (4.6) by –7, one can also derive the relationships that say how many sharps or flats a given key signature has.

$$Sharps \equiv 7 \times MinorKey \ (mod \ 12) \qquad (4.7)$$

$$Flats \equiv -7 \times MinorKey \ (mod \ 12) \qquad (4.8)$$

The Circle of Fifths

The *Circle of Fifths* is a common visual representation for equations (4.5) and (4.6). Figure 4-6 shows a visual representation of the note numbers with the major keys in the outside circle and the minor keys in the inside circle. To relate sharps to key signature, one starts at the top position of **C** and goes over a clockwise number of increments equal to the number of sharps. For flats, the same thing is done in a counterclockwise direction. Technically, one could consider a key signature expressed either in number of flats or number of sharps, but for purposes of naming key signatures, there is a preference to the smaller number. For instance, the key of **F** can be said to have 1 flat or 11 sharps, but musicians would choose the simpler way and just say it has one flat.

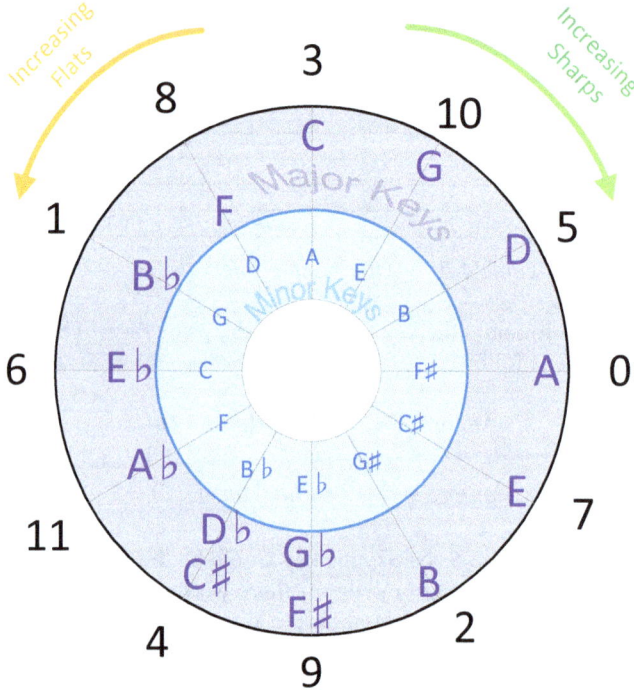

Figure 4-6   The Circle of Fifths

Chapter 5

Higher Order Modulus Equations

Introduction

Not all things behave exactly the same way for modular arithmetic as they do in conventional algebra when dealing with powers not equal to one. For instance, some positive numbers have no square roots, while others can have more than two square roots. Another oddity is that two numbers can have a product that is zero without either one of them being zero, when the modulus is not prime. This foils the factoring concept in solving equations of higher order. As a result, many of the solution methods for linear and algebraic equations do not work for modulus equations of higher order. That being said, there are some more routine methods that work when the modulus is prime and also the reduction of modulus theorem is useful in many cases when it is not.

Modulus Equations of Prime Modulus

Most of the elegant results come when the modulus is prime for higher order equations involving the modulus operator. One key result that can be used is the following theorem.

Theorem 5.1   Factorization Theorem

Suppose that **P** is prime and that $x_1, x_2, \ldots x_n \equiv 0 \pmod{P}$.
Then at least one of $x_1, x_2, \ldots x_n$ must be zero **mod P**.

Proof

Suppose x_1 is zero, then the theorem is satisfied. Otherwise, divide through by x_1 and to get the result that $x_2, \ldots x_n \equiv 0 \pmod{P}$. This process can be repeated until at least one of these coefficients is zero or the equation simplifies to $x_n \equiv 0 \pmod{P}$. It is important for **P** to be prime, otherwise the modulus could get divided down after we divide through by all these terms.

The Factorization Theorem allows equations to be factored and solved. For example, suppose that:

$$(x-2) \cdot (x-3) \equiv 0 \pmod{13} \tag{5.1}$$

Because 13 is a prime number, the solution to this equation is:

$$x \equiv 2, 3 \pmod{13} \tag{5.2}$$

Factoring with Modular Arithmetic of Prime Modulus

Factoring with modular arithmetic is very similar to factoring with traditional algebra, except it involves the modulus operator and is done over the set of integers. Equation (5.3) shows a polynomial that is factored in modular arithmetic so that the equation can be solved.

$$x^2 + 11 \cdot x + 4 \equiv (x-7) \cdot (x-8) \equiv 0 \pmod{13} \tag{5.3}$$

Although (5.3) might show the solution, it would be desirable to have a more systematic method to factor polynomials. One method that is useful is that if one of the roots of the polynomial is known, it can be divided out to simplify the polynomial. In other words, if *x=a* is a solution, then *x–a* factors the polynomial. This is done the same way as in algebraic expressions and is best illustrated by example. Realize that this only works with a prime modulus.

Example

Given that *x=1* is a solution to the following equation, factor this to out to find the other solutions.

$$2 \cdot x^3 + 3 \cdot x^2 + 10 \cdot x + 11 \equiv 0 \pmod{13} \tag{5.4}$$

Since *x=1* is a solution, then *x–1* is a factor. Also realize that any multiple of 13 can be added or subtracted to simplify the equation.

$$\begin{array}{r}
2 \cdot x^2 + 5 \cdot x + 2 \\
x-1 \overline{\smash{\big)}\, 2 \cdot x^3 + 3 \cdot x^2 + 10 \cdot x + 11} \\
\underline{2 \cdot x^3 - 2 \cdot x^2} \\
5 \cdot x^2 + 10 \cdot x \\
\underline{5 \cdot x^2 - 5 \cdot x} \\
2 \cdot x + 11 \\
\underline{2 \cdot x - 2} \\
0
\end{array} \tag{5.5}$$

So now we can say that:

$$\begin{aligned} 2 \cdot x^3 + 3 \cdot x^2 + 10 \cdot x + 11 \\ \equiv (x-1) \cdot (2 \cdot x^2 + 5 \cdot x + 2) \equiv 0 \pmod{13} \end{aligned} \tag{5.6}$$

By observation, we see that 6 is also a solution to (5.6), so *x – 6* is a factor that can be divided out.

$$\begin{array}{r} 2\cdot x+4 \\ x-6 \overline{\smash{\big)}\,2\cdot x^2 + 5\cdot x+2} \\ \underline{2\cdot x^2 - 12\cdot x} \\ 4\cdot x+2 \\ \underline{4\cdot x-24} \\ 0 \end{array} \qquad (5.7)$$

Note that this can be expressed modulo 13 as:

$$2\cdot(x-11) \qquad (5.8)$$

So we can ultimately factor this as:

$$\begin{aligned}&2\cdot x^3 + 3\cdot x^2 + 10\cdot x + 11 \\ &\equiv 2\cdot(x-1)\cdot(x-6)\cdot(x-11) \equiv 0 \ (\bmod\ 13)\end{aligned} \qquad (5.9)$$

So 1, 6, and 11 are the solutions to (5.9). In general, n^{th} degree polynomial, it can have up to n roots in modular arithmetic with prime modulus, but it could have less than this.

Solving Equations that do not have a Prime Modulus

So far, the focus has been on equations where the modulus is prime, because this is the case for which more elegant solution methods exist. When the modulus is not prime, a good strategy is to use the reduction of modulus theorem (Theorem 3.3) to simplify the equation into one with prime modulus. This equation can be solved with the extraneous roots removed, or be shown to have no solution. For example, consider the following equation:

$$5\cdot x^2 + 3\cdot x \equiv 7 \ (mod\ 10) \qquad (5.10)$$

The reduction of modulus theorem can be used to show that if a solution exists to (5.10), it must also solve (5.11).

$$x^2 + x \equiv 1 \ (mod\ 2) \qquad (5.11)$$

Because (5.11) has no solutions, there will be no solutions to (5.10). For cases where there is a solution, the methods often resemble an intelligent trial and error. Consider the following equation that demonstrates this.

$$5 \cdot x^2 + 3 \cdot x + 9 \equiv 0 \ (mod\ 161) \tag{5.12}$$

Note that 161 is a multiple of 7 and 23 and is therefore not prime. Using reduction of modulus, a simpler equation can be found.

$$5 \cdot x^2 + 3 \cdot x + 2 \equiv 0 \ (mod\ 7) \tag{5.13}$$

By trial and error, we can see that the solution to (5.13) is 2. This means the possible solutions to (5.12) would be 2, 9, 16, …154. Trying these solutions, we see that the ones that work are 44, 52, 121, and 136.

The temptation may be to try to factor out the 44 and reduce the equation to find the other solutions, but one should be very cautious in doing this as the equation does not have a prime modulus. To illustrate that this does not work completely, let's try this out as in (5.14) to see what happens.

$$\begin{array}{r} 5 \cdot x + 62 \\ x - 44 \overline{\smash{\big)}\ 5 \cdot x^2 + 3 \cdot x + 9} \\ \underline{5 \cdot x^2 - 220 \cdot x } \\ 62 \cdot x + 9 \\ \underline{62 \cdot x - 2728} \\ 0 \end{array} \tag{5.14}$$

The solution to (5.14) is 52, which is a correct solution, but the problem is that we have lost the other solutions of 121 and 136.

Example
Suppose that Robert is planning a backyard patio as shown in Figure 5-1. The patio is to consist of 2 large squares with a 2 foot gap to plant plants. On each side of this gap, he wants a one block wide walkway. Also, on the side closest to the house, he wants one more row of blocks. He is using 1 foot square blocks that are $10/each or sold in packs 10 for $80. It is desired to use a perfect multiple of 10 blocks to get the most value for the money and to have no waste. How can this project be done so that it is done with a perfect multiple of 10 blocks?

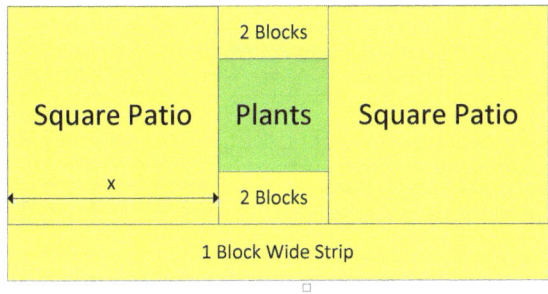

Figure 5-1   *Patio Example*

Solution
Adding up the blocks required we get:

2 Square Patios:	$2 \cdot x^2$
1 Block Wide Strip:	$2 \cdot x + 2$
2 Sets of 2 Blocks by Plants:	4
Grand Total:	$2 \cdot x^2 + 2 \cdot x + 6$

So the equation to solve is:

$$2 \cdot x^2 + 2 \cdot x + 6 \equiv 0 \;(mod\; 10) \qquad (5.15)$$

One can divide through by two in order to reduce this equation.

$$x^2 + x + 3 \equiv 0 \;(mod\; 5) \qquad (5.16)$$

By inspection, we can see that 1 and 3 are the solutions to (5.15). Values for *x* that correspond to this are 1,3,6,8,11,13,16,17, ... One reasonable solution might be to choose *x=11* as a solution, which would correspond to 270 blocks.

Square Roots in Modular Arithmetic

Square roots in modular arithmetic are the solutions to the following equation.

$$x^2 \equiv a \;(mod\; M) \qquad (5.17)$$

If *M* modulus is prime, then there will either be two square roots (one positive and one negative) or no square roots. For cases where the modulus is not prime, it is possible for there to be more than two square roots.

		Number																												
		0	1	2	3	4	5	6	7	8	9	10	11	12	13	14	15	16	17	18	19	20	21	22	23	24	25	26	27	28	29
Modulus	1	0																													
	2	0	1																												
	3	0	1																												
	4	0,2	1																												
	5	0	1			2																									
	6	0	1	3	2																										
	7	0	1	3		2																									
	8	0,4	1,3			2																									
	9	0,3	1			2			4																						
	10	0	1			2	5	4			3																				
	11	0	1		5	2	4				3																				
	12	0,6	1,5			2,4					3																				
	13	0	1		4	2					3	6		5																	
	14	0	1	4		2			7	6	3		5																		
	15	0	1,4			2,7		6			3	5																			
	16	0,4,8	1,7			2,6					3,5																				
	17	0	1	6		2				5	3				8		7	4													
	18	0,6	1			2		5			3,9	8		7			4														
	19	0	1			2	9	5	8		3	7					4	6													
	20	0,10	1,9			2,8	5				3,7						4,6														
	21	0	1,8			2,5			7		3						6	4,10		9											
	22	0	1	5	2	7					3		11	10		6	9	4				8									
	23	0	1	5	7	2		11		10	3			9	6		4		8												
	24	0,12	1,5,7,11			2,10					3,9			6			4,8														
	25	0,5,10	1			2		9			3		6			8			12			11			7						
	26	0	1	9	2						3	6		8	13	12		4	11			10	7		5						
	27	0,9	1			2			13		3,6,12	8		11				4			10		7		5						
	28	0,14	1,13			2,12				6,8	3,11						4,10				7				5,9						
	29	0	1			2	11	8	6		3		10				4				7		14	9	13	5		12			
	30	0	1,11			2,8		6			3	10					15	4,14			7,13		9			12	5				

Table 5-3   Modular Square Roots

Powers in Modular Arithmetic

Powers in modular arithmetic are somewhat straightforward. One elegant result is Fermat's Little Theorem, which follows.

Theorem 5.2   *Fermat's Little Theorem*

If p is prime then $x^{p-1} \equiv 1 \ (mod \ p)$ and $x^p \equiv x \ (mod \ p)$.

Proof

Consider the product $(1 \cdot x) \cdot (2 \cdot x) ... ((p-1) \cdot x) \equiv 1 \cdot 2 \cdot ... \cdot (p-1) \cdot x^{p-1} \ (mod \ p)$. Because p is prime and $1 \cdot 2 \cdot ... \cdot (p-1)$ has no common factors with p then Theorem 3.4 says that we can just divide out this common factor from both sides to get the result that $x^{p-1} \equiv 1 \ (mod \ p)$, which can be multiplied by both sides to get the result that $x^p \equiv x \ (mod \ p)$.

For example this theorem could be used to show that $16^{23} \ mod \ 23 = 16$. This can be used to reduce down powers as well. For example, if we have $6^{13} \ mod \ 7$, we call pull off the first 6 powers an say that this is the same as $6^7 \ mod \ 7$, which is 6.

Chapter 6

Diophantine Equations

Introduction

Diophantine equations are equations of at least two variables that only have integer solutions. The fact that solutions are restricted to integers allows them to be solved with fewer constraints than typical algebraic equations. Many of the techniques for modulus equations discussed so far can be used to also solve Diophantine equations. There are many kinds of Diophantine equation, but the first order linear equation (6.1) is one of the most common and also has well established solution methods.

$$a \cdot x + b \cdot y = c \qquad (6.1)$$

Theorem 6.1 *Linear Diophantine Equation Solution Existence and Uniqueness*

For **a,b,** and **c** integers, the equation **a·x + b·y = c** has a solution if and only if **c** is a multiple of the greatest common divisor of **a** and **b**. If this is the case, there are infinitely many solutions.

Proof

If one takes both sides of this equation modulo **GCD (a, b)** then this shows why **GCD(a, b)** must divide **c** for a solution to exist. Given that this condition is satisfied, one can divide through by **GCD(a, b)** and take both sides of the equation modulo **b** to get a resulting linear modulus equation that has a solution as shown in Theorem 3.5. Because this is a modular equation, one can add any multiple of the modulus to a solution to get another solution.

Examples:
$2 \cdot x + 3 \cdot y = 5$ has infinitely many integer solutions because the greatest common divisor of 2 and 3 is 1, and 5 is a multiple of 1.

$6 \cdot x + 3 \cdot y = 5$ has no integer solutions because the greatest common divisor of 6 and 3 is 3, yet 5 is not a multiple of 3.

Finding the Homogeneous Solution

The initial step in solving (6.1) is to first simplify the equation and determine if a solution exists at all. If so, then it is necessary to find the homogeneous solution, that is the case for when $c=0$. This solution is easy to find. Consider the equation:

$$a \cdot x + b \cdot y = 0 \qquad (6.2)$$

If we assume that a and b have no common factors (if they do, just divide them out), then the solution to this is:

$$\begin{pmatrix} x \\ y \end{pmatrix} = k \cdot \begin{pmatrix} b \\ -a \end{pmatrix} \qquad (6.3)$$
$$k = 0, \pm 1, \pm 2, \dots$$

Example
Solve the following equation:

$$3 \cdot x + 5 \cdot y = 0 \qquad (6.4)$$

The solution is:

$$\begin{pmatrix} x \\ y \end{pmatrix} = k \cdot \begin{pmatrix} 5 \\ -3 \end{pmatrix} \qquad (6.5)$$
$$k = 0, \pm 1, \pm 2, \dots$$

Finding the Particular Solution

Once the homogenous solution is known, then all that is needed is to find any solution that satisfies the equation when the right hand side is not zero. The simplest case happens when one of the coefficients is one. In this case, just plug in zero for the variable accompanying the nonzero coefficient and solve, as shown in the following example:

$$x + b \cdot y = c \qquad (6.6)$$

Since 0 is an integer, substitute it in for y to get a particular solution of:

$$\begin{pmatrix} x_p \\ y_p \end{pmatrix} = \begin{pmatrix} c \\ 0 \end{pmatrix} \qquad (6.7)$$

If neither of the coefficients is one, then one strategy is to use the modulus operator to eliminate one of the variables and then solve the resulting modular equation.

Example
Find a particular solution to:

$$23 \cdot x + 16 \cdot y = 29 \qquad (6.8)$$

Take both sides modulo 16 to get:

$$7 \cdot x \equiv 13 \pmod{16} \qquad (6.9)$$

Using the methods already presented and multiplying both sides by 7 (which is the inverse of 7 modulo 16), the following result is obtained.

$$x \equiv 11 \pmod{16} \qquad (6.10)$$

Although x could assume values of 11,27,43..., one can just use the value of 11 because increasing x by 16 is the same as increasing y by one. Substituting this back in (6.8) allows y to be found.

$$23 \cdot 11 + 16 \cdot y = 29$$
$$y = \frac{29 - 11 \cdot 23}{16} = -14 \qquad (6.11)$$

Applying Restrictions to Solutions of Diophantine Equations

Many integer equations arise from very practical solutions where further restrictions can be applied that can reduce the number of solutions, or even narrow the range of solutions to a unique solution. Since integers arise a lot in counting, one common restriction is that none of the integers can be negative. If this still does not narrow the solution, another popular restriction is how one variable relates to another.

Example
At a school function, two meals are offered. The prices including tax are $6.29 for the adult meal and $1.04 for the kid's meal. Total receipts for sales total $115.25. How many of each type of meals were sold?

Solution

Let **x** be the number of adult meals sold and **y** be the number of kids meals sold. If the sales are expressed in terms of cents, the equation is:

$$629 \cdot x + 104 \cdot y = 11525 \tag{6.12}$$

Since there are no common factors there is a solution. The homogeneous solution is:

$$\begin{pmatrix} x_H \\ y_H \end{pmatrix} = \begin{pmatrix} 104 \\ -629 \end{pmatrix} \cdot k \tag{6.13}$$

$$k = 0, \pm 1, \pm 2, \ldots$$

The particular solution can be found by taking the equation modulus 104.

$$629 \cdot x + 104 \cdot y = 11525$$

$$5 \cdot x_P \equiv 85 \pmod{104}$$

$$x_P = 17 \tag{6.14}$$

$$y_P = \frac{11525 - 629 \cdot 17}{104} = 8$$

The complete solution is therefore:

$$\begin{pmatrix} x \\ y \end{pmatrix} = \begin{pmatrix} x_H \\ y_H \end{pmatrix} + \begin{pmatrix} x_P \\ y_P \end{pmatrix} = \begin{pmatrix} 17 \\ 8 \end{pmatrix} + \begin{pmatrix} 104 \\ -629 \end{pmatrix} \cdot k \tag{6.15}$$

$$k = 0, \pm 1, \pm 2, \ldots$$

Now it is time to apply the restriction that we know that we cannot sell any negative numbers of meals. If k was greater than zero, then this would be a negative number of kid's meals. If k was less than zero, then this would be a negative number of adult meals. It therefore follows that **k=0**, which implies that 17 adult meals and 8 kids meals were sold.

Example

A fruit stand sells only apples and mangoes. Including taxes, apples sell for $0.51 each and mangoes sell for $1.03 each. At the end of the day, receipts for the sales of these two fruits are $117.98. The seller at the fruit stand lost count, but could say that there were "many times" more apples sold than mangoes. How many apples and how many oranges were sold?

Solution

Let x be the number of apples sold and y be the number of mangoes sold. If the sales are expressed in terms of cents, the equation is:

$$51 \cdot x + 103 \cdot y = 11798 \qquad (6.16)$$

A solution exists because there are no common factors there is a solution. The homogeneous solution is as follows.

$$\begin{pmatrix} x_H \\ y_H \end{pmatrix} = \begin{pmatrix} 103 \\ -51 \end{pmatrix} \cdot k \qquad (6.17)$$
$$k = 0, \pm 1, \pm 2, \ldots$$

The particular solution can easily be found by taking the equation modulus 51.

$$y \equiv 11798 \pmod{17}$$
$$y_P = 17$$
$$x_P = \frac{11798 - 103 \cdot 17}{51} = 197 \qquad (6.18)$$

The complete solution is therefore:

$$\begin{pmatrix} x \\ y \end{pmatrix} = \begin{pmatrix} x_H \\ y_H \end{pmatrix} + \begin{pmatrix} x_P \\ y_P \end{pmatrix} = \begin{pmatrix} 197 \\ 17 \end{pmatrix} + \begin{pmatrix} 103 \\ -51 \end{pmatrix} \cdot k \qquad (6.19)$$
$$k = 0, \pm 1, \pm 2, \ldots$$

Now it is time to apply the restriction that we know that we cannot sell any negative numbers of fruits. The first constraint is that we know that we cannot sell a negative number of apples. For both quantities to be positive, we can see that $k = 0,1$. The solution corresponding to $k=0$ is that 197 apples and 17 mangoes sold. The solution corresponding to $k=1$ is that 94 apples and 68 mangoes were sold. Since the fruit stand seller knew that there were "many times" more apples than mangoes sold, this narrows the solution to 197 apples sold and 17 mangoes.

Equations of 2 or More Variables with Size Restrictions

There are many situations where a whole is expressed in terms of smaller pieces. One good example of this is if we want to express time in terms of seconds, minutes, hours, days, months, and years. Each larger quantity is a multiple of the next largest quantity. The solution method is obvious in this example, but there are similar situations that might use the same solution method where this calculation might not be as familiar. To generalize this example, consider the following equation, where $x_0 \ldots x_n$ are unknowns and $a_0 \ldots a_n$ are known constants.

$$\sum_{n=0}^{k} a_n \cdot x_n = R \qquad (6.20)$$

Assume the following restrictions which apply for $0 \leq n \leq k-1$:

$$0 \leq a_n < a_{n+1}$$
$$a_{n+1} \equiv 0 \pmod{a_n} \qquad (6.21)$$

This equation can easily be solved regardless of how many variables. In order to solve this type of solution, one can either choose by starting at x_0 and working their way to x_k or, go the other way. Applying the modulus operator can quickly find the first unknown:

$$x_0 = R \bmod a_1 \qquad (6.22)$$

The next step is to subtract x_0 from both sides and then divide through by a_1.

$$x_1 = \frac{(R - a_0)}{a_1} \bmod \left(\frac{a_2}{a_1}\right) \qquad (6.23)$$

This process can be repeated for any number of variables. The last variable can be found algebraically, but a faster way is to divide through and just find the remainder.

$$x_k = floor\left(\frac{M}{a_k}\right) \qquad (6.24)$$

Example
Express 10000 seconds in terms of hours, minutes, and seconds.

Solution
We need to solve the equation:

$$3600 \cdot hour + 60 \cdot min + sec = 10000 \qquad (6.25)$$

The seconds can be easily found.

$$sec = 10000 \bmod 60 = 40 \qquad (6.26)$$

Once this is done, the minutes can also be found.

$$60 \cdot hour + min = \frac{10000 - 40}{60}$$
$$min = 166 \bmod 60 = 46 \qquad (6.27)$$

Finally, hours can just be found algebraically:

$$3600 \cdot hour + 60 \cdot 46 + 40 = 10000$$
$$hour = 2 \qquad (6.28)$$

Now although most people could probably do this type of problem without any familiarity with diophantine equations at all, it is very common to miss applying these simple concepts to equations when not dealing with something less familiar than time

Example
As a magic trick, ask someone to pick 3 whole numbers between 0 and 9 inclusive. Add the first two numbers. Now add 9 times the first number to that sum. Next add 13 to the whole sum. Now multiply the whole sum by 10. From that subtract 11. Now add the third number.

After the answer is given, you can immediately recite what the three original numbers were. If we call the numbers x, y, and z then this whole expression can be calculated as follows:

$$10 \cdot (x + y + 9 \cdot x + 13) - 11 + z = 100x + 10y + z + 119 \qquad (6.29)$$

The secret is to subtract 119 from the result. After this is done, the numbers will show up in the digits of the answer.

Linear Diophantine Equations of More than 2 Variables

The techniques for linear Diophantine equations can be used to find solutions for higher order equations.

Finding the Homogeneous Solution
Consider the equation $a_1 x_1 + \ldots + a_n x_n \equiv 0$. The homogeneous solution can be constructed in a very similar way as when there were 2 variables. Set all but terms 1 and 2 to zero and find the basis with this. Then do the same with terms 2 and 3, and so on. In this way, the basis is easy to find.

Example
Find the solution of:

$$x + 3 \cdot y - 2 \cdot z = 0 \qquad (6.30)$$

The solution is shown below, where **s** and **t** are integers.

$$\begin{pmatrix} x \\ y \\ z \end{pmatrix} = s \cdot \begin{pmatrix} 3 \\ -1 \\ 0 \end{pmatrix} + t \cdot \begin{pmatrix} 0 \\ 2 \\ 3 \end{pmatrix} \qquad (6.31)$$

Finding the Complete Solution

Theorem 6.2   *Linear Equation Theorem of Many Variables*
For the integers $a_1, a_2, \ldots a_n$ and c, the equation $a_1 x_1 + \ldots + a_n x_n \equiv c$ has infinitely many solutions if and only if c is a multiple of the greatest common divisor of $a_1, a_2, \ldots a_n$.

Proof
    First establish that c would have to be a multiple of the greatest common divisor of $a_1, a_2, \ldots a_n$. This is rather intuitive because if the greatest common divisor divides $a_1, a_2, \ldots a_n$, then if these terms are multiplied by integers and combined, the result would also have to be a multiple of this greatest common divisor.
    Now suppose that c is a multiple of the greatest common divisor of $a_1, a_2, \ldots a_n$.   First divide out this common factor.   Within the resulting linear combination, one will be able to find or create two variables that are relatively prime. If it did not directly result from the division, then variables with a common factor could be combined into a new variable.   The common factor can not be common to all of the variables because the greatest common divisor has been divided out.   Since there is a linear combination involving two relatively prime numbers, this can produce any integer and therefore infinitely many solutions exist as proven in Theorem 6.1.

Solution Techniques

The first thing to do is divide out any common factors, since this greatly simplifies the math. So from now forth, it will be assumed that there are no common factors. Now if any two or more terms have a common factor that is not shared with the others, then factor these out and redefine the variable.

Example
Find the integer solutions of:

$$2 \cdot x + 6 \cdot y + 7 \cdot z = 41 \tag{6.32}$$

Solution
Now for the homogeneous solution, take two different pairs from the 3 variables for the basis.

$$\begin{pmatrix} x_H \\ y_H \\ z_H \end{pmatrix} = s \cdot \begin{pmatrix} 6 \\ -2 \\ 0 \end{pmatrix} + t \cdot \begin{pmatrix} 0 \\ 7 \\ -6 \end{pmatrix} \tag{6.33}$$

To find the particular solution, just choose any integer for x, y, or z. Zero is a convenient choice. The only caution is that you have to make sure that the resulting equation of two variables is solvable. In this case, choose $x=0$ to get:
$$6 \cdot y + 7 \cdot z = 41 \tag{6.34}$$

Take both sides modulo 6 to get:

$$z \equiv 5 \pmod{6} \tag{6.35}$$

Substituting this back in, we can easily find y, so the particular solution is:

$$\begin{pmatrix} x_P \\ y_P \\ z_P \end{pmatrix} = \begin{pmatrix} 0 \\ 1 \\ 5 \end{pmatrix} \tag{6.36}$$

The complete solution is therefore:

$$\begin{pmatrix} x \\ y \\ z \end{pmatrix} = \begin{pmatrix} 0 \\ 1 \\ 5 \end{pmatrix} + s \cdot \begin{pmatrix} 6 \\ -2 \\ 0 \end{pmatrix} + t \cdot \begin{pmatrix} 0 \\ 7 \\ -6 \end{pmatrix} \tag{6.37}$$

This same solution technique could be expanded to any number of variables.

Frobenius Equations

Frobenius equations are linear diophantine equations where the solutions are restricted to nonnegative values and are of the form:

$$a_1 \cdot x_1 + a_2 \cdot x_2 + \ldots a_n \cdot x_n = b \tag{6.38}$$

The techniques presented so far can be used to solve these equations when b is known, but of particular interest is the *Frobenius Number*, which is the largest value of b for which equation (6.38) has no solution. For this number to exist, the following restriction is necessary.

$$GCD(a_1, a_2, \ldots, a_n) = 1 \tag{6.39}$$

For the case that $n=1$ in (6.38), the problem is trivial and for the case that $n > 2$, no closed form solution is known. However, for the case that $n=2$, the 19th Century British mathematician James Sylvester found an elegant formula:

$$b_{max} = a_1 \cdot a_2 - a_1 - a_2 \tag{6.40}$$

One well known application of this formula *coin problem* that considers the largest denomination that cannot be made from two coins. For instance, if there were two coins denomination 5 and 7, then the largest value that could not be created by this would be 23. Another way of expressing (6.40) is to find the next higher value, which represents the smallest value of the value of the continuous range that can be synthesized.

$$b_{max} + 1 = (a_1 - 1) \cdot (a_2 - 1) \tag{6.41}$$

One application (6.41) is *dual modulus prescalers*, which are commonly used in high frequency applications to synthesize larger divider values. To do this, a fixed prescaler of value P and other circuitry are used that can create any divide value that is a linear combination of P and $P+1$ to create a total divide value of N as follows.

$$N = a_1 \cdot P + a_2 \cdot (P+1) \tag{6.42}$$

Of special interest is the *minimum continuous divide ratio*, above which any value of N can be created. This can be found by (6.41) to be:

$$N_{min} = (P-1) \cdot (P+1-1) = P \cdot (P-1) \tag{6.43}$$

For example, a 16/17 prescaler can synthesize any continuous range N divide values, provided the smallest one is 240 or larger.

Nonlinear Diophantine Equations

Nonlinear equations tend to have less elegant and less standard solution methods. Aside from dividing out common factors, sometimes applying the modulus operator can give insight. For example, taking modulo 3 of the equation $3x^2 + 9y = 7$ can quickly show that there are no integer solutions. Following are a few famous nonlinear diophantine equations.

Pythagorean Triples

Pythagorean triples are positive integer solutions to the following equation.

$$x^2 + y^2 = z^2 \tag{6.44}$$

If *(a,b,c)* is a solution, the we can multiply all three of these by a positive integer and it will also be a solution. For this reason, *Primitive Pythagorean Triples*, are those with no common factors, the first several sets are shown below:

(3, 4, 5)	(5, 12, 13)	(8, 15, 17)	(7, 24, 25)
(20, 21, 29)	(12, 35, 37)	(9, 40, 41)	(28, 45, 53)
(11, 60, 61)	(16, 63, 65)	(33, 56, 65)	(48, 55, 73)
(13, 84, 85)	(36, 77, 85)	(39, 80, 89)	(65, 72, 97)

Reference [1] gives the formula for these triples. To do this, choose positive integers *m* and *n* such that they have no common factors, their difference is odd, and *m* is greater than *n*. From this, all the triples can be generated as shown below.

$$\left(2 \cdot m \cdot n, m^2 - n^2, m^2 + n^2\right) \tag{6.45}$$

Fermat's Last Theorem

The theorem states that for any integer, $n > 2$, there are no whole numbers that satisfy the following equation:

$$x^n + y^n = z^n \tag{6.46}$$

It's not that this equation has great application, but rather it looks deceptively simple to solve. Fermat claimed to have an elegant proof for this that would not fit on the margin of his page, but many question if he really had such a proof. The actual proof was done using very abstract concepts like elliptic curves by Wiles and is discussed in [2]. However, the proof was so long and so abstract, this could not possibly have been the proof that Fermat says was "elegant". Many a mathematician has wasted countless hours thinking that they would be the one to find this elegant proof, including the author. Taking that in mind, it would probably be best to discuss something else instead of getting lured into spending more time on futile attempts to finding an elegant solution to Fermat's Last Theorem.

Pell's Equation

A less famous equation in number theory is Pell's equation that seeks integer solutions to:

$$x^2 - a \cdot y^2 = 1 \tag{6.47}$$

This equation does have solutions and is discussed in reference [3].

References

[1]   Joyce, D. E. (June 1997), "Book X, Proposition XXIX", Euclid's Elements, *Clark University*

[2]   Singh, Simon   Fermat's Enigma: The Epic Quest to Solve the World's Greatest Mathematical Problem. Copyright 1997, Simon Singh.

[3]   Barbeau, Edbard J.   Pell's Equation   Copyright 2003, Springer-Verlag New York, Inc.

From Differential Equations to Difference Equations

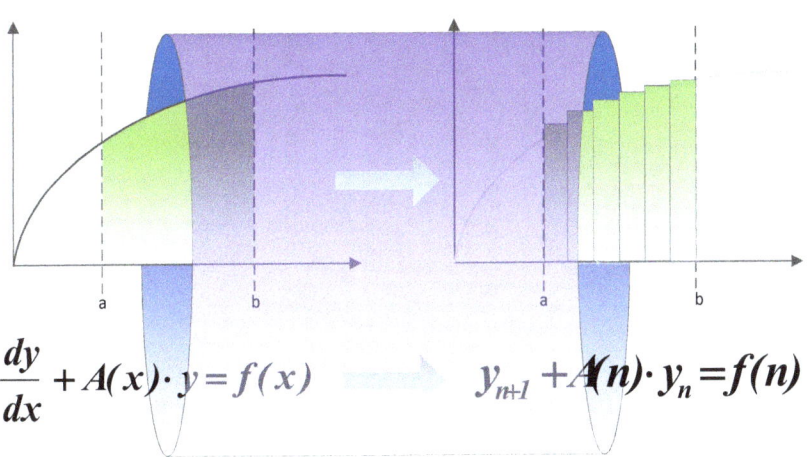

$$\frac{dy}{dx} + A(x) \cdot y = f(x) \quad \longrightarrow \quad y_{n+1} + A(n) \cdot y_n = f(n)$$

Chapter 7

Finite Differences, Sums, and Products

Introduction

Finite differences, sums, and products are key concepts in solving difference equations. Finite differences and sums can be thought of the discrete equivalents to derivatives and integrals that are used in calculus.

Finite Differences and their Similarities to Derivatives

In calculus, the concept of taking a derivative starts with a function, *y(x)*. For this function, one chooses an arbitrary point, *(x, y(x))* and then another point *(x + Δx, y(x + Δx))*. A visual representation of this is shown in Figure 7-1.

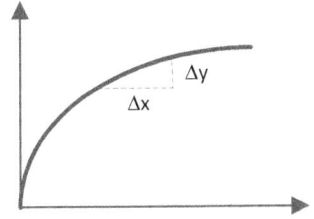

Figure 7-1   *Concept of a Derivative*

If we consider the limit as *Δx* approaches zero, then we get the definition of derivative in (7.1).

$$derivitave = \lim_{\Delta x \to 0} \left(\frac{y(x + \Delta x) - y(x)}{\Delta x} \right)$$

$$= \lim_{\Delta x \to 0} \left(\frac{\Delta y}{\Delta x} \right) = \frac{dy}{dx} \quad (7.1)$$

dx represents the infinitesimally small quantity as *Δx* approaches zero, and *dy* represents how much the function changes over this infinitesimally small quantity. For example, calculate the derivative of x^2:

$$slope = \lim_{\Delta x \to 0} \left(\frac{(x + \Delta x)^2 - x^2}{\Delta x} \right) = \lim_{\Delta x \to 0} \left(\frac{2 \cdot \Delta x + \Delta x^2}{\Delta x} \right) = 2 \cdot x \quad (7.2)$$

The formulas shown here are technically the right hand derivative, because it approaches the final value from the right. Provided that the function is smooth, it does not matter if Δx approaches zero from a negative or a positive value.

Finite differences are very similar to derivatives except that $\Delta x \to 1$. For this book, the focus will be on using the right hand finite difference.

$$Finite\, Difference = \frac{\Delta y}{\Delta x} = \Delta y = \frac{y_{n+1} - y_n}{1} = y_{n+1} - y_n \qquad (7.3)$$

The finite difference is has many similarities with derivatives. For example, consider the derivative rule for a power.

$$\frac{d}{dx} x^k = k \cdot x^{k-1} \qquad (7.4)$$

The equivalent rule for finite differences is similar, but slightly different. For instance, the finite difference of n^2 is $2 \cdot n + 1$, not $2 \cdot n$. In order to "fix" this to look more like the derivative rule, the equivalent statement is:

$$\begin{aligned}
\Delta \left(\frac{n!}{(n-k)!} \right) &= \frac{(n+1)!}{(n+1-k)!} - \frac{n!}{(n-k)!} \\
&= \frac{n!}{(n-k)!} \cdot \left(\frac{n+1}{n+1-k} - 1 \right) \\
&= \frac{k}{n-1-k} \cdot \frac{n!}{(n-k)!} = k \cdot \frac{n!}{(n-k-1)!}
\end{aligned} \qquad (7.5)$$

Another similarity between finite differences and derivatives is the exponent rule. Consider the derivatives of the exponential and power functions.

$$\frac{d}{dx} e^x = e^x \qquad (7.6)$$

$$\frac{d}{dx} k^x = \ln(k) \cdot k^x \qquad (7.7)$$

The equivalent rule for finite differences is (7.8).

$$\Delta k^n = (k-1) \cdot k^n \qquad (7.8)$$

Comparing (7.6) to (7.8), it suggests that **2** acts like the discrete equivalent **e** as the natural logarithm base. Table 7-3 shows some finite differences and equivalent derivative expressions.

Expression	Finite Difference	Derivative Equivalent
n	1	$\frac{d}{dx}x = 1$
n^2	$2 \cdot n + 1$	$\frac{d}{dx}x^2 = 2 \cdot x$
n^3	$3 \cdot n^2 + 3 \cdot n + 1$	$\frac{d}{dx}x^3 = 3 \cdot x$
$n \cdot (n-1)$	$2 \cdot n$	$\frac{d}{dx}x^2 = 2 \cdot x$
$n \cdot (n-1) \cdot (n-2)$	$3 \cdot n \cdot (n-1)$	$\frac{d}{dx}x^3 = 3 \cdot x$
$\frac{n!}{(n-k)!}$	$k \cdot \frac{n!}{(n+1-k)!}$	$\frac{d}{dx}x^k = k \cdot x^{k-1}$
2^n	2^n	$\frac{d}{dx}e^x = e^x$
k^n	$(k-1) \cdot k^n$	$\frac{d}{dx}k^x = ln(k) \cdot k^x$

Table 7-3 *Various Finite Differences*

Higher Order and Larger Step Finite Differences

Higher order finite differences are analogous to higher order derivatives and can be calculated by applying the finite difference operation multiple times. For example, the second order finite difference can be calculated by taking the finite difference two times.

$$\Delta^2 y_n = \Delta y_{n+1} - \Delta y_n = y_{n+2} - 2 \cdot y_{n+1} + y_n \qquad (7.9)$$

The third order finite difference can be calculated as the finite difference of the second order finite difference.

$$\begin{aligned}\Delta^3 y_n &\equiv \Delta^2 y_{n+1} - \Delta^2 y_n \\ &= (y_{n+3} - 2 \cdot y_{n+2} + y_{n+1}) - (y_{n+2} - 2 \cdot y_{n+1} + y_n) \\ &= y_{n+3} - 3 \cdot y_{n+2} + 3 \cdot y_{n+1} - y_n\end{aligned} \qquad (7.10)$$

The trend that (7.9) and (7.10) are suggesting is the general (7.11) that can easily be proved by mathematical induction.

$$\Delta^k y_n = \sum_{i=0}^{k}(-1)^{k-i} \cdot \binom{k}{i} \cdot y_{n+i} \qquad (7.11)$$

Larger step finite differences are when the difference is more than one index apart. These may be expressed in terms of the sum of single step finite differences, as shown in Table 7-4.

Larger Step Finite Difference	Equivalent Expression
$y_{n+1} - y_n$	-
$y_{n+2} - y_n$	$\Delta y_{n+1} + \Delta y_n$
$y_{n+3} - y_n$	$\Delta y_{n+2} + \Delta y_{n+1} + \Delta y_n$
$y_{n+k} - y_n$	$\sum_{i=0}^{k-1} \Delta y_{n+i}$

Table 7-4 *Higher Order Finite Differences*

The Discrete Analogy to the Product Rule for Finite Differences

The product rule from calculus allows one to find the derivative of two functions, *f(x)* and *g(x)* and is shown below:

$$(f(x) \cdot g(x))' = f'(x) \cdot g(x) + g'(x) \cdot f(x) \quad (7.12)$$

For example, the derivative of x^2 can be calculated as

$$(x \cdot x)' = 1 \cdot x + x \cdot 1 = 2 \cdot x \quad (7.13)$$

For finite differences, the analogous rule is similar, but slightly different because the left and right finite differences are not the same.

$$\begin{aligned}\Delta(u_n \cdot v_n) &= u_{n+1} \cdot v_{n+1} - u_n \cdot v_n \\ &= u_{n+1} \cdot v_{n+1} - u_{n+1} \cdot v_n + u_{n+1} \cdot v_n - u_n \cdot v_n \\ \Rightarrow \Delta(u_n \cdot v_n) &= u_{n+1} \cdot \Delta v_n + v_n \cdot \Delta u_n \end{aligned} \quad (7.14)$$

Finite Sums

Relating Finite Sums to the Integral

The *finite sum* has many similarities with the integral, which relates to the area under the curve. The concept of the integral is to divide the area into a large amount of pieces of width Δx and then add up all the pieces. The smaller Δx is, the closer the summation will be to the true area. If we take the limit as this width approaches zero, then it becomes the true area.

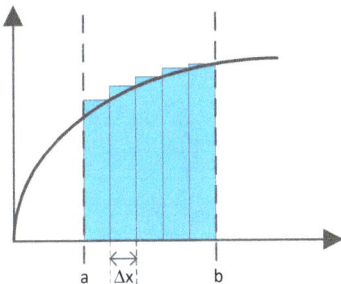

Figure 7-2   *Approximating an Integral with a Finite Sum*

The integral is related to the area under the curve as follows:

$$\int_a^b y \cdot dx \equiv \lim_{\Delta x \to 0} \left(\sum_{n=0}^{\frac{b-a}{\Delta x}} y(a + n \cdot \Delta x) \cdot \Delta x \right) \quad (7.15)$$

The concept of summation is very similar to integration except that $\Delta x = 1$ as shown in (7.16).

$$\left(\sum_{n=0}^{\frac{b-a}{\Delta x}} y(a + n \cdot \Delta x) \cdot \Delta x \right)\bigg|_{\Delta x = 1} = \sum_{n=0}^{b-a} y(a+n) = \sum_{n=a}^{b} y(n) \quad (7.16)$$

In some situations where the finite sum is not easy to calculate, the integral can be used to approximate it as in (7.17). For this approximation, the approximation is fairly close and only slightly less than the true sum.

$$\sum_{n=4}^{100} \sqrt{n} = 667.3167 \ldots$$

$$\int_4^{100} \sqrt{x} \cdot dx = \frac{2}{3} \cdot x^{3/2} \bigg|_4^{100} = 661.\overline{3} \quad (7.17)$$

Table 7-5 shows some common finite sums. For this table, the lower summation limit is not given so these finite sums could vary by an arbitrary constant. Also, because some of the functions, they might not be defined at $n=0$, so the summation typically starts at $n=1$.

Function	Finite Sum to 1 to N	Related Concept
Δy_n	$y_{N+1} - y_1$	Telescoping Series
$\Delta f(y_n)$	$f(y_{N+1}) - f(y_1)$	
$\dfrac{1}{n \cdot (n+1)}$	$\dfrac{N}{N+1}$	
$a + n \cdot d$	$a \cdot N + \dfrac{N \cdot (N+1) \cdot d}{2}$	Arithmetic Series
1	N	
n	$\dfrac{N \cdot (N+1)}{2}$	
n^2	$\dfrac{N \cdot (N+1) \cdot (2N+1)}{6}$	Power Series
n^3	$\dfrac{N^2 \cdot (N+1)^2}{4}$	
$\dfrac{n!}{(n-k)!},\ n > 1$	$\dfrac{(n+1)!}{(n-k)! \cdot k}$	Inverse of Equation (7.5)
$2 \cdot n$	$(n+1) \cdot n$	
$3 \cdot n \cdot (n-1)$	$(n+1) \cdot n \cdot (n-1)$	
$4 \cdot n \cdot (n-1) \cdot (n-2)$	$(n+1) \cdot n \cdot (n-1) \cdot (n-2)$	
r^{n-1}	$\dfrac{1 - r^N}{1 - r}$	Geometric Series
$(n-1) \cdot r^{n-2}$	$\dfrac{1 - N \cdot r^{N-1}}{(1-r)^2}$	Derivative of Geometric Series
$\cos(n \cdot \alpha)$	$\dfrac{\sin[(N+0.5) \cdot \alpha]}{2 \cdot \sin[0.5 \cdot \alpha]} - \dfrac{1}{2}$	Trigonometric Series
$\sin(n \cdot \alpha)$	$\dfrac{\sin[0.5 \cdot (N+1) \cdot \alpha] \cdot \sin[0.5 \cdot N \cdot \alpha]}{\sin[0.5 \cdot \alpha]}$	
$\log(n)$	$\log(N!)$	Logarithmic Series

Table 7-5   *Finite Sums*

The finite sums in Table 7-5 are useful in solving difference equations. For the other results, it is possible to make many more formulae for finite sums by taking linear combinations, derivatives, or using summation by parts. One other consideration is that when Δy_n is summed N, the result is y_{N+1}. It is for this reason that difference equations are sometimes summed to $N-1$ so that the result is y_N.

Summation by Parts

Recall that from calculus, the integration by parts rule is given as follows:

$$\int_a^b f(x) \cdot g'(x) \cdot dx = f(x) \cdot g(x) - \int g(x) \cdot f'(x) \cdot dx \tag{7.18}$$

The derivation of this rule involves taking the product rule (7.12) and integrating both sides.

$$\begin{aligned}
&\tfrac{d}{dx}(f(x) \cdot g(x)) = f'(x) \cdot g(x) + g'(x) \cdot f(x) \\
&\Rightarrow f(x) \cdot g(x) = \int f'(x) \cdot g(x) \cdot dx + \int f(x) \cdot g'(x) \cdot dx \\
&\Rightarrow \int f(x) \cdot g'(x) \cdot dx = f(x) \cdot g(x) - \int g(x) \cdot f'(x) \cdot dx
\end{aligned} \tag{7.19}$$

By applying the summation operator to both sides of (7.14), the summation by parts rule can be derived, which is analogous to the integration by parts rule (7.19) for calculus.

$$\begin{aligned}
\sum_{n=a}^{b} \Delta(u_n \cdot v_n) &= \sum_{n=a}^{b} v_{n+1} \Delta u_n + \sum_{n=a}^{b} u_n \Delta v_n \\
u_n \cdot v_n \Big|_{n=a}^{n=b+1} &= \sum_{n=a}^{b} v_{n+1} \Delta u_n + \sum_{n=a}^{b} u_n \Delta v_n
\end{aligned} \tag{7.20}$$

Rearranging the equation yields the rule for summation by parts:

$$\sum_{n=a}^{b} u_n \cdot \Delta v_n = u_n \cdot v_n \Big|_{n=a}^{n=b+1} - \sum_{n=a}^{b} v_{n+1} \cdot \Delta u_n \tag{7.21}$$

Example
For example, (7.21) can be used to find the sum of a standard arithmetic series.

$$\begin{aligned}
\sum_{n=0}^{k} n &= u_n \cdot v_n \Big|_{n=0}^{n=k+1} - \sum_{n=0}^{k} (n+1) \cdot 1 = \\
\Rightarrow \sum_{n=0}^{k} n &= \frac{k \cdot (k+1)}{2}
\end{aligned} \tag{7.22}$$

Building on (7.22), it is possible to expand this to the sum of squares applying (7.21).

$$\sum_{n=0}^{k} n^2 = (k+1)^3 - \sum_{n=0}^{k}(n+1)\cdot(2n+1)$$

$$\Rightarrow \sum_{n=0}^{k} n^2 = (k+1)^3 - (k+1) - 3\frac{k\cdot(k+1)}{2} - 2\sum_{n=0}^{k} n^2$$

$$\Rightarrow \sum_{n=0}^{k} n^2 = \frac{2\cdot(k+1)^3 - 2\cdot(k+1) - 3k\cdot(k+1)}{6}$$

$$\Rightarrow \sum_{n=0}^{k} n^2 = \frac{k\cdot(k+1)\cdot(2k+1)}{6}$$

(7.23)

Finite Products

Aside from finite differences and finite sums, finite products also sometimes come up when solving difference equations. The *finite product* is defined as follows:

$$\prod_{n=0}^{N} y_n \equiv y_0 \cdot y_1 \cdot \ldots \cdot y_N \qquad (7.24)$$

The following table shows some common finite products.

Function	Finite Product from 1 to N
$\dfrac{y_{n+1}}{y_n}$	$\dfrac{y_{N+1}}{y_1}$
$\dfrac{y_{n+k}}{y_n}$	$\dfrac{y_{N+k}}{y_1}$
$\dfrac{\Delta y_n}{y_n}+1$	$\dfrac{y_{N+1}}{y_1}$
k	k^N
n	$N!$

Table 7-6   Finite Products

Conclusion

This chapter has related finite sums and difference and sums to derivates and integrals. These form the fundamental building blocks in order to solve difference equations. Finite products do not have such a similar analogy in calculus, but are also very useful for solving difference equations, especially first order ones.

Chapter 8

First Order Difference Equations

Introduction

First order difference equations are those that involve only the first order finite difference. Provided that the equations are linear, there exist general methods that will always work. This chapter starts with some more simple cases and then deals with the more complicated general case.

Solution Method of For Homogeneous Equations

A *homogeneous equation* is one where the right hand side is zero as shown below.

$$y_{n+1} - A(n) \cdot y_n = 0 \tag{8.1}$$

This equation can be written as follows.

$$\frac{y_{n+1}}{y_n} = A(n) \tag{8.2}$$

By taking a finite product of both sides, the equation can be solved.

$$y_n = \prod_{k=1}^{n-1} A(k) \tag{8.3}$$

The following example shows a solution using this method.

$$y_{n+1} - \frac{n+1}{n} \cdot y_n = 0$$

$$\Rightarrow \frac{y_{n+1}}{y_n} = \frac{n+1}{n} \tag{8.4}$$

$$\Rightarrow y_n = \prod_{k=1}^{n-1} \frac{k+1}{k} = y_1 \cdot n$$

Constant Coefficient Solution Method

For the case that $A(n)$ is a constant, the substitution of (8.5) always works.

$$u_n \cdot A^{n-1} \to y_n \tag{8.5}$$

For example, consider the following equation:

$$y_{n+1} - 2 \cdot y_n = 3^n \tag{8.6}$$

The first step is to make the substitution (8.7).

$$u_n \cdot 2^{n-1} \to y_n \tag{8.7}$$

The resulting steps to the solution are in (8.8).

$$u_{n+1} \cdot 2^n - 2 \cdot u_n \cdot 2^{n-1} = 3^n$$
$$2^n \cdot \Delta u_n = 3^n$$
$$\sum_{k}^{n-1} \Delta u_k = u_n = \sum_{k=0}^{n-1} \left(\frac{3}{2}\right)^k = \frac{1 - \left(\frac{3}{2}\right)^n}{1 - \frac{3}{2}} = 2 \cdot \left(\left(\frac{3}{2}\right)^n - 1\right) \tag{8.8}$$

This series leads to the solution for u_n with c defined as an arbitrary constant.

$$u_n = 2 \cdot \left(\left(\frac{3}{2}\right)^n - 1\right) + \hat{c} = 2 \cdot \left(\frac{3}{2}\right)^n + 2 \cdot c \tag{8.9}$$

Substituting (8.9) into (8.7) yields the final solution.

$$y_n = 3^n + c \cdot 2^n \tag{8.10}$$

General Solution Method

The linear first order difference equation is any equation of the form:

$$y_{n+1} - A(n) \cdot y_n = f(n) \tag{8.11}$$

There is no loss of generality in assuming the highest order term is equal to one, since one could just divide through by this coefficient. In general, equation (8.11) will have a unique solution provided that there is an initial condition specified. The following substitution will reduce (8.11) to an equation that can be solved.

$$u_n \cdot \prod_{k=0}^{n-1} A(k) \to y_n \qquad (8.12)$$

Substituting (8.12) into (8.11) yields the following:

$$u_{n+1} \cdot \prod_{k=0}^{n} A(k) - A(n) \cdot u_n \cdot \prod_{k=0}^{n-1} A(k) = f(n) \qquad (8.13)$$

Equation (8.13) can be simplified as follows.

$$\Delta u_n = \frac{f(n)}{\prod_{k=0}^{n} A(k)} \qquad (8.14)$$

Equation (8.14) can be solved for u_n and then (8.12) can be applied to find the final solution for y_n.

Consider the following example:

$$y_{n+1} - n \cdot y_n = \alpha \qquad (8.15)$$

Use the substitution:

$$u_n \cdot (n-1)! \to y_n \qquad (8.16)$$

This leads the following solution steps:

$$\begin{aligned} u_{n+1} \cdot n! - n \cdot (n-1)! \cdot u_n &= \alpha \\ \Delta u_n \cdot n! &= \alpha \end{aligned} \qquad (8.17)$$

$$u_n = c + \alpha \cdot \sum_{k=1}^{n-1} \frac{1}{k!} \qquad (8.18)$$

Combining (8.16) and (8.18) yields the final solution.

$$y_n = \alpha \cdot (n-1)! + \alpha \cdot (n-1)! \cdot \sum_{k=1}^{n-1} \frac{1}{k!} \qquad (8.19)$$

For this particular equation, $y_1 = \alpha$ because we see this is true when $n = 0$ in the original equation.

In general, the first order equation will have one constant that can be specified by an initial condition. In the previous example, we also see that sometimes y_0 is not defined and we have to start the summation at y_1.

Nonlinear First Order Equations

The methods for nonlinear equations tend to be more equation specific. Some nonlinear equations can be solved by means of doing a substitution that reduces it into an equation that can be solved as is shown in (8.20).

$$(n+1)\cdot y_{n+1}^2 - n\cdot y_n^2 = 1 \tag{8.20}$$

The substitution that works for this equation is:

$$z_n \to n\cdot y_n^2 \tag{8.21}$$

This reduces (8.20) to a linear equation that can be solved.

$$\begin{aligned}\Delta z_n &= 1 \\ z_n &= n+c\end{aligned} \tag{8.22}$$

Combining (8.21) and (8.22) yields the final result.

$$y_n = \pm\sqrt{1+\frac{c}{n}} \tag{8.23}$$

Conclusion

Provided that the equation is linear, first order difference equations can be solved in a straightforward manner using the methods shown, although it could lead to an expression involving a summation that does not have a closed form. Nonlinear equations have their own personality and need to be treated more on a case by case basis.

Chapter 9

Methods for Higher Order Difference Equations

Introduction

For higher order equations, methods exist for the cases where the coefficients are all constant as well as the case where an existing solution is known. This chapter discusses these two methods.

Constant Coefficient Equations

An example of a second order constant coefficient difference equation is shown in (9.1). This example might be second order, but the method will really work for any order constant coefficient equation.

$$y_{n+2} + a_1 \cdot y_{n+1} + a_0 \cdot y_n = 0 \tag{9.1}$$

The solution methods to solving this equation are very similar to those used for constant coefficient differential equations. The approach is to assume a solution of the form $y_n = r^n$, and substitute into (9.1), which results in solving an algebraic equation as shown in (9.2).

$$r^2 + a_1 \cdot r + a_0 = 0$$
$$\Rightarrow r_{0,1} = \frac{-a_1 \pm \sqrt{a_1^2 - 4 \cdot a_0}}{2} \tag{9.2}$$

There are three situations that could happen for these roots r_0 and r_1; they could be real and distinct, complex and distinct, or a real and the same. For the first the case of two real distinct roots, y_n is a linear combination of these two solutions.

$$y_n = c_0 \cdot (r_0)^n + c_1 \cdot (r_1)^n \tag{9.3}$$

For example, consider the following example:

$$y_{n+2} - 2 \cdot y_{n+1} - 3 \cdot y_n = 0$$
$$\Rightarrow r_{0,1} = -1, 3 \tag{9.4}$$
$$y_n = c_0 \cdot (-1)^n + c_1 \cdot 3^n$$

Another possibility for the roots in (9.2) could be that the roots are distinct and complex. This can be treated exactly the same as two real and distinct roots, but for cosmetic purposes, it is sometimes desirable to use *Euler's identity* as shown in (9.5).

$$e^{i \cdot x} = \cos(x) + i \cdot \sin(x) \tag{9.5}$$

Euler's identity can be used to combine these roots in a different linear combination involving the sine and cosine functions. Consider the following example

$$y_{n+2} + 2 \cdot y_{n+1} + 2 \cdot y_n = 0$$

$$\Rightarrow r_{0,1} = \frac{-2 \pm \sqrt{2^2 - 4 \cdot 2}}{2} = -1 \pm i$$

$$y_n = c_0 \cdot (-1+i)^n + c_1 \cdot (-1-i)^n \tag{9.6}$$

$$= \left(\sqrt{2}\right)^n \cdot e^{i \cdot \frac{3\pi \cdot n}{4}} + \left(\sqrt{2}\right)^n \cdot e^{-i \cdot \frac{3\pi \cdot n}{4}}$$

$$= d_0 \cdot \left(\sqrt{2}\right)^n \cdot \cos\left(\frac{3\pi \cdot n}{4}\right) + d_1 \cdot \left(\sqrt{2}\right)^n \cdot \sin\left(\frac{3\pi \cdot n}{4}\right)$$

The third and final case in (9.2) is that there is only one root, which will be real. In this case, the other root will be *n* times the original root. The derivation for this result is in the appendix. Example (9.7) shows an illustration of the case where there is only one root.

$$y_{n+2} - 2 \cdot k \cdot y_{n+1} + k^2 \cdot y_n = 0$$

$$\Rightarrow t_{0,1} = \frac{2 \cdot k \pm \sqrt{(2 \cdot k)^2 - 4 \cdot k^2}}{2} = k \tag{9.7}$$

Because there is only a single root, the solution is:

$$y_n = c_0 \cdot (k)^n + c_1 \cdot n \cdot (k)^n \tag{9.8}$$

Reduction of Order

When one of the roots is known in a linear difference equation, the reduction of order method can be used to reduce it. The derivations and examples to higher order equations are shown in the appendix, but the second order equation illustrates the general concept. Consider the second order equation (9.9).

$$y_{n+2} + a_1(n) \cdot y_{n+1} + a_0(n) \cdot y_n = 0 \tag{9.9}$$

Suppose that f_n is a solution to (9.9). The first step is to express y_n as the product as the known solution and an unknown solution as in (9.10).

$$y_n = x_n \cdot f_n \qquad (9.10)$$

A substitution of (9.10) into (9.9) yields the following expression for x_n.

$$x_{n+2} \cdot f_{n+2} + a_1(n) \cdot x_{n+1} \cdot f_{n+1} + a_0(n) \cdot x_n \cdot f_n = 0 \qquad (9.11)$$

Another expression can be obtained by substituting f_n into (9.9) and multiplying through by x_n.

$$x_n \cdot f_{n+2} + x_n \cdot a_1(n) \cdot f_{n+1} + x_n \cdot a_0(n) \cdot f_n = 0 \qquad (9.12)$$

Expression (9.13) is obtained by subtracting (9.12) from (9.11).

$$f_{n+2} \cdot (x_{n+2} - x_n) + a_1(n) \cdot f_{n+1} \cdot (x_{n+1} - x_n) = 0 \qquad (9.13)$$

Now do the following substitution on (9.13).

$$w_n \rightarrow x_{n+1} - x_n \qquad (9.14)$$

This leads to the following expression.

$$f_{n+2} \cdot (w_{n+1} + w_n) + a_1(n) \cdot f_{n+1} \cdot w_n = 0 \qquad (9.15)$$

After some rearranging, the final result is obtained.

$$f_{n+2} \cdot w_{n+1} + (f_{n+2} + a_1(n) \cdot f_{n+1}) \cdot w_n = 0 \qquad (9.16)$$

One of the solutions to (9.16) is $w_n=0$, but this solution will reduce (9.9) to an equation that is solved by the known solution. The other solution will lead to a new equation of lower order that yields the other solution. For higher order equations, this technique can be expanded. The case of the third order equation is handled in the appendix. As an illustration of how to use this method, consider the following equation:

$$y_{n+2} - 2 \cdot \frac{n+1}{n+2} \cdot y_{n+1} + \frac{n}{n+2} \cdot y_n = 0 \qquad (9.17)$$

Note that any constant satisfies the equation. Choose this constant to be equal to *1* and combine the results from (9.16) and (9.17) to form a simplified equation.

$$w_{n+1} + \left(-2 \cdot \frac{n+1}{n+2} + 1\right) \cdot w_n = 0$$

$$\frac{w_{n+1}}{w_n} = \frac{n}{n+2} \tag{9.18}$$

$$w_n = \prod_{k=1}^{n-1} \frac{k}{k+2} = \frac{2}{3} \cdot \frac{1}{n \cdot (n+1)}$$

The other solution can be found by summing up (9.18). Realize that because this is a linear difference equation, one can multiply the solution by any constant and it will still be a solution. What this means is the factor of 2/3 can be dropped if desired.

$$y_n = \sum_{k=1}^{n-1} \frac{1}{k \cdot (k+1)} = \sum_{k=1}^{n-1} \left[\frac{1}{k} - \frac{1}{k+1}\right] = 1 - \frac{1}{n} \tag{9.19}$$

The two solutions can be combined in order to create the total solution to (9.17) that is shown below.

$$y_n = c_0 + \frac{c_1}{n} \tag{9.20}$$

Finding the Particular Solution

So far only homogenous equations have been considered. For linear difference equations that are not homogeneous that have a right hand side that is nonzero, finding the homogenous solution is the first step. After this is found, the next step is to find any solution that satisfies the right hand side of the equation, called the particular solution. The total solution is the sum of the particular and the homogenous solutions. The general way to find a particular solution is to use methods that involve an educated and flexible guess, which will now be discussed.

The Method of Undetermined Coefficients

The *method of undetermined coefficients* is the same as used in differential equations and involves making an educated guess containing some variables so that it has a higher likelihood of working.

For example, consider equation (9.21).

$$y_{n+3} + 3 \cdot y_{n+2} - 2 \cdot y_{n+1} + y_n = 18 \qquad (9.21)$$

A simple guess would be to try:

$$yp_n = k \qquad (9.22)$$

Substituting this in the original equation yields the particular solution.

$$k + 3 \cdot k - 2 \cdot k + k = 18$$
$$yp_n = 6 \qquad (9.23)$$

In general, a guess of a constant will work on any constant coefficient linear equation that has a right hand side that is constant. In general, guessing a particular solution that is a multiple of the expression on the right hand side of the equation is a good approach as shown in Table 9-3.

Right Hand Side	Guess Solution of
c (constant)	k (constant)
r^n	$k \cdot r^n$
N	$a_1 \cdot n + a_0$
$\sum_{i=0}^{k} a_i \cdot n^i$ (i.e. any polynomial)	$\sum_{i=0}^{k} b_i \cdot n^i$ (same order polynomial with different coefficients)

Table 9-3   *Particular Solution Guesses*

For constant coefficient equations, even if guessing a multiple of the right hand side is not the correct answer, it can sometimes lead to the correct answer as in (9.24).

$$y_{n+2} - 5 \cdot y_{n+1} + 6 \cdot y_n = n \qquad (9.24)$$

For this equation, a potential first guess could be:

$$yp_n = a \cdot n \qquad (9.25)$$

Substituting this in yields the following:

$$n \cdot (a - 5 \cdot a + 6 \cdot a) - 3 \cdot a = n \tag{9.26}$$

If we choose **a=1/2**, then the result is close, but there is still a residual constant. To fix this, the original guess can be modified to:

$$yp_n = \frac{n}{2} + b \tag{9.27}$$

The result of substituting this in has all the terms involving **n** cancel, yielding the particular solution.

$$\frac{n+2}{2} + b - \frac{5}{2} \cdot (n+1) - 5 \cdot b + 3 \cdot n + 6 \cdot b = n$$
$$b = 3/4 \tag{9.28}$$
$$yp_n = \frac{n}{2} + \frac{3}{4}$$

Conclusion

The methods for solving homogeneous equations, reduction of order, and the method of undetermined coefficients all involve making an intelligent guess at the form of the solutions. Although guessing might sound like a random strategy, these guesses have variables in them to make them cover more general situations, which make them more like a solution method.

Appendix: Derivations of Various Results

Derivation that Second Root is n Times the First Root for the Constant Coefficient Equation with Repeated Roots

Consider the equation (9.29) and assume that it has a repeated root.

$$y_{n+2} + a_1 \cdot y_{n+1} + a_0 \cdot y_n = 0 \quad (9.29)$$

One assumes a solution of the form $y_n = r^n$, and substitute this in, the result is:

$$r^2 + a_1 \cdot r + a_0 = 0$$

$$\Rightarrow r = \frac{-a_1 \pm \sqrt{a_1^2 - 4 \cdot a_0}}{2} \quad (9.30)$$

But since the root is repeated, we can say that:

$$a_1^2 - 4 \cdot a_0 = 0 \quad (9.31)$$

$$r = \frac{-a_1}{2} \quad (9.32)$$

Consider the solution of:

$$y_n = n \cdot \left(\frac{-a_1}{2}\right)^n \quad (9.33)$$

Substituting (9.33) into (9.29) and applying (9.31) shows that this is a solution also.

$$(n+2) \cdot \left(\frac{-a_1}{2}\right)^{n+2} + a_1 \cdot (n+1) \cdot \left(\frac{-a_1}{2}\right)^{n+1} + a_0 \cdot n \cdot \left(\frac{-a_1}{2}\right)^n$$

$$= \frac{1}{4} \cdot \left(\frac{-a_1}{2}\right)^n \cdot \left\{(n+2) \cdot a_1^2 - 2 \cdot (n+1) \cdot a_1^2 + 4 \cdot a_0 \cdot n\right\} \quad (9.34)$$

$$= \frac{1}{4} \cdot \left(\frac{-a_1}{2}\right)^n \cdot n \cdot 2 \cdot \left(-a_1^2 + 4 \cdot a_0\right) = 0$$

For the case of higher order difference equations that have a repeated root, the resulting polynomial for t can be factored as a quadratic expression times a polynomial and a similar result can be found. In the case that there is a root repeated more than once, then this rule applies to finding one of the other roots, but not the others.

Reduction of Order for a Third Order Equation

A third order equation can be stated as follows:

$$y_{n+3} + a_2(n) \cdot y_{n+2} + a_1(n) \cdot y_{n+1} + a_0(n) \cdot y_n = 0 \tag{9.35}$$

Suppose that we know that f_n satisfies this equation.

$$f_{n+3} + a_2(n) \cdot f_{n+2} + a_1(n) \cdot f_{n+1} + a_0(n) \cdot f_n = 0 \tag{9.36}$$

Write the next unknown solution as the product of the known solution times an unknown solution.

$$y_n = x_n \cdot f_n \tag{9.37}$$

Substituting this in we get:

$$\begin{aligned} x_{n+3} \cdot f_{n+3} + a_2(n) \cdot x_{n+2} \cdot f_{n+2} \\ + a_1(n) \cdot x_{n+1} \cdot f_{n+1} + a_0(n) \cdot x_n \cdot f_n = 0 \end{aligned} \tag{9.38}$$

Multiplying (9.36) by x_n and subtracting it from (9.38) yields the following equation.

$$\begin{aligned} f_{n+3} \cdot (x_{n+3} - x_n) + a_2(n) \cdot f_{n+2} \cdot (x_{n+2} - x_n) \\ + a_1(n) \cdot f_{n+1} \cdot (x_{n+1} - x_n) = 0 \end{aligned} \tag{9.39}$$

Make the following substitution.

$$w_n = x_{n+1} - x_n \tag{9.40}$$

This substitution yields the second order equation that is one order lower than the original equation.

$$\begin{aligned} f_{n+3} \cdot w_{n+2} + (f_{n+3} + a_2(n) \cdot f_{n+2}) \cdot w_{n+1} \\ + (f_{n+3} + a_2(n) \cdot f_{n+2} + a_1(n) \cdot f_{n+1}) \cdot w_n = 0 \end{aligned} \tag{9.41}$$

This method could be expanded to any order linear homogenous equation above third order by using a similar method of reasoning.

Chapter 10

Systems of Ordinary Difference Equations

Introduction

When there are multiple interrelated variables and an equal number of equations, this is considered to be a system of equations. One example of a system of equations is as follows.

$$\begin{aligned} x_{n+1} &= x_n + y_n + 1 \\ y_{n+1} &= -2 \cdot x_n + 4 \cdot y_n + 2 \end{aligned} \tag{10.1}$$

One approach to solving this would be to take the first equation and solve for y_n and substitute into the second equation as shown in (10.2). This equation can be solved for x_n and the result from this can be used to find y_n.

$$\begin{aligned} y_n &= x_{n+1} - x_n - 1 \\ x_{n+2} - x_{n+1} - 1 &= -2 \cdot x_n + 4 \cdot (x_{n+1} - x_n - 1) + 2 \\ \Rightarrow x_{n+2} - 5 \cdot x_{n+1} + 6 \cdot x_n &= -1 \end{aligned} \tag{10.2}$$

This method of substitution is effective and intuitive, although it can lead to higher order equations. An alternative way of expressing equations (10.1) is using matrix operations as in (10.3).

$$\begin{bmatrix} x_{n+1} \\ y_{n+1} \end{bmatrix} = \begin{bmatrix} 1 & 1 \\ -2 & 4 \end{bmatrix} \bullet \begin{bmatrix} x_n \\ y_n \end{bmatrix} + \begin{bmatrix} 1 \\ 2 \end{bmatrix} \tag{10.3}$$

Expressing the equations in matrix form allows them to be written in a more elegant and compact form. In order to solve this kind of equation using matrices, some familiarity with matrix algebra is required. This chapter has a brief review of matrix mathematics and then shows how this can be used to solve systems of difference equations.

Brief Review of Matrix Mathematics

Matrix Dimensions and Multiplication

A *m* x *n* matrix is a collection of numbers in *m* rows and *n* columns. If *m=n*, the matrix is said to be a *square matrix*. Matrices can only be multiplied if the inner dimensions match. For instance, a 6 × 2 matrix can be multiplied by a 2 × 6 matrix to create a 6 × 6 matrix, but they cannot be multiplied the other way; matrix multiplication is not commutative. The element in row *x* and column *y* of the product is found by taking the dot product of row *x* of the first matrix and column *y* of the second matrix.

$$\begin{bmatrix} a & b \\ c & d \end{bmatrix} \bullet \begin{bmatrix} e & f \\ g & h \end{bmatrix} = \begin{bmatrix} a \cdot e + b \cdot g & a \cdot f + b \cdot h \\ c \cdot e + d \cdot g & c \cdot f + d \cdot h \end{bmatrix} \quad (10.4)$$

For matrix algebra, there exists the multiplicative identity matrix which is commonly denoted as *I*. This matrix has 1's down the diagonal and zeroes elsewhere. Any matrix can be multiplied by this and be unchanged, provided the dimensions of this match.

Determinants
The *determinant* is a number that only applies to square matrices and will be nonzero if and only if the inverse for the matrix exists. The determinant for a 2 × 2 matrix is shown in (10.5).

$$\begin{vmatrix} a & b \\ c & d \end{vmatrix} = a \cdot d - b \cdot c \quad (10.5)$$

In general, if there are all zero entries above or below the diagonal of a matrix, then the determinant is the product of these entries. For any arbitrary matrix, multiples of rows or columns can be subtracted or added to other rows or columns without changing the determinant. Using this property, the determinant of a matrix can be found as is done in the following example.

$$\begin{vmatrix} 1 & 8 & 1 \\ 2 & 5 & 7 \\ 4 & 5 & 2 \end{vmatrix} \quad (10.6)$$

Subtract twice row 2 from row 3. Then subtract twice row 1 from row 2.

$$\begin{vmatrix} 1 & 8 & 1 \\ 0 & -11 & 5 \\ 0 & -5 & -12 \end{vmatrix} \quad (10.7)$$

Subtract 5/11 row 2 from row 3.

$$\begin{vmatrix} 1 & 8 & 1 \\ 0 & -11 & 5 \\ 0 & 0 & -157/11 \end{vmatrix} = 1 \times (-11) \times (-157/11) = 157 \quad (10.8)$$

Matrix Inverses

The inverse of a matrix A, denoted A^{-1}, exists when the determinant is nonzero and gives the identity matrix when multiplied by A. One way of calculating the inverse is to start with the original matrix on the left side and the identity matrix on the right side. The matrix on the left side is then reduced to the identity matrix by multiplying rows by constants and subtracting away multiples of other rows. The remaining matrix on the right will be the inverse. This method is illustrated in the following example.

$$\begin{bmatrix} 1 & 1 \\ -2 & 4 \end{bmatrix} \Leftrightarrow \begin{bmatrix} 1 & 0 \\ 0 & 1 \end{bmatrix} \tag{10.9}$$

Add twice the first row to the second row:

$$\begin{bmatrix} 1 & 1 \\ 0 & 6 \end{bmatrix} \Leftrightarrow \begin{bmatrix} 1 & 0 \\ 2 & 1 \end{bmatrix} \tag{10.10}$$

Divide the second row by 6:

$$\begin{bmatrix} 1 & 1 \\ 0 & 1 \end{bmatrix} \Leftrightarrow \begin{bmatrix} 1 & 0 \\ \frac{1}{3} & \frac{1}{6} \end{bmatrix} \tag{10.11}$$

Subtract the second row from the first to get the inverse:

$$\begin{bmatrix} 1 & 0 \\ 0 & 1 \end{bmatrix} \Leftrightarrow \begin{bmatrix} \frac{2}{3} & -\frac{1}{6} \\ \frac{1}{3} & \frac{1}{6} \end{bmatrix} \tag{10.12}$$

Eigenvectors and Eigenvalues

Given a matrix, there are a set of vectors that have the unique property that when multiplied by the matrix, the vector only changes magnitude, but not angle. In other words, given a matrix, A, and a vector, $\vec{x}$, the following equation is satisfied.

$$A \bullet \vec{x} = \lambda \bullet \vec{x} \tag{10.13}$$

λ is said to be the *eigenvalue* and $\vec{x}$ is said to be the *eigenvector*. Once an eigenvector is found, any scalar multiple of that will also satisfy the equation. For this reason, and to make this easier to apply to later subjects, it will be assumed that eigenvectors are normalized to unit length. Although the zero vector satisfies this equation, it is not considered an eigenvector. These can be calculated by solving a system of linear equations. To do this, rewrite (10.13) as follows.

$$(A - \lambda \bullet I) \bullet \vec{x} = 0 \tag{10.14}$$

If the matrix $(A - \lambda \bullet I)$ has a nonzero determinant, then one could just multiply through by its inverse and then all the eigenvectors would be zero, which are not very interesting. The only way for (10.14) to have nonzero eigenvectors is the determinant is zero and (10.15) is satisfied. This will lead to a set of algebraic equations that can be solved for the eigenvalues, which will lead to another system of equations that can be used to find the eigenvectors.

$$|A - \lambda \bullet I| = 0 \tag{10.15}$$

To illustrate this technique, define the matrix A as shown below. This particular matrix will be used in several examples throughout the chapter.

$$A = \begin{bmatrix} 1 & 1 \\ -2 & 4 \end{bmatrix} \tag{10.16}$$

Applying (10.15) leads to the algebraic equations for the eigenvalues.

$$\begin{vmatrix} 1-\lambda & 1 \\ -2 & 4-\lambda \end{vmatrix} = 0 \tag{10.17}$$

Calculating the determinant leads the following algebraic equation and solution.

$$(1-\lambda) \cdot (4-\lambda) + 2 = 0$$
$$\lambda = 2, 3 \tag{10.18}$$

From these eigenvalues, the eigenvectors can be calculated from the null space by substituting in the eigenvalues into (10.17). For example, for the eigenvalue of 2, the substitution is done.

$$\begin{bmatrix} -1 & 1 \\ -2 & 2 \end{bmatrix} \bullet \begin{pmatrix} x \\ y \end{pmatrix} = \begin{pmatrix} 0 \\ 0 \end{pmatrix} \tag{10.19}$$

This gives the constraint that $x = y$, which leads to the following eigenvector.

$$\vec{x}_1 = \begin{bmatrix} 1 \\ 1 \end{bmatrix} \tag{10.20}$$

A similar exercise can be done for the eigenvalue of 3.

$$\begin{bmatrix} -2 & 1 \\ -2 & 1 \end{bmatrix} \bullet \begin{pmatrix} x \\ y \end{pmatrix} = \begin{pmatrix} 0 \\ 0 \end{pmatrix} \tag{10.21}$$

This leads to a solution of $y = 2x$, which in turn leads to the other eigenvector.

$$\vec{x}_2 = \begin{bmatrix} 1 \\ 2 \end{bmatrix} \tag{10.22}$$

Diagnolizing a Matrix
Given a matrix, A, it desirable to write it in the form (10.23).

$$A = S \bullet D \bullet S^{-1} \tag{10.23}$$

It is not always possible to do this, but one sufficient condition would be if the matrix had all distinct eigenvalues. The matrix, S is formed by taking the eigenvectors of M as columns. The matrix D is formed by putting the eigenvalues down the diagonal of this matrix and making the other entries zero. The matrix S^{-1} can be found by using the methods already presented. It can easily be shown that the product of matrices (10.24), (10.25), and (10.26) yields the original matrix A that was defined in (10.16).

$$S = \begin{bmatrix} 1 & 1 \\ 1 & 2 \end{bmatrix} \tag{10.24}$$

$$D = \begin{bmatrix} 2 & 0 \\ 0 & 3 \end{bmatrix} \tag{10.25}$$

$$S^{-1} = \begin{bmatrix} 2 & -1 \\ -1 & 1 \end{bmatrix}. \tag{10.26}$$

Powers of a Matrix
If a matrix can be diagnolized and expressed in form (10.23), then calculating powers of a matrix involve calculating the powers of the eigenvalues.

$$\begin{aligned} A^n &= \left(S \bullet D \bullet S^{-1}\right)^n \\ &= S \bullet D \bullet S^{-1} \bullet S \bullet D \bullet S^{-1} \ldots \bullet S \bullet D \bullet S^{-1} \\ &= S \bullet D^n \bullet S^{-1} \end{aligned} \tag{10.27}$$

Referring back to (10.23) and its elements of (10.24), (10.25), and (10.26), powers of this matrix can be simplified.

$$A^n = \begin{bmatrix} 1 & 1 \\ 1 & 2 \end{bmatrix} \cdot \begin{bmatrix} 2^n & 0 \\ 0 & 3^n \end{bmatrix} \cdot \begin{bmatrix} 2 & -1 \\ -1 & 1 \end{bmatrix}$$

$$= \begin{bmatrix} 2^{n+1} - 3^n & 3^n - 2^n \\ 2^{n+1} - 2 \cdot 3^n & 2 \cdot 3^n - 2^n \end{bmatrix} \quad (10.28)$$

Solving the Homogeneous First Order System

Now that matrices have been reviewed, it is time to apply them to difference equations. The homogeneous first order system can be expressed in matrix form as shown.

$$\vec{y}_{n+1} - A \cdot \vec{y}_n = 0 \quad (10.29)$$

The solution to this system is elegantly expressed in terms of powers of a matrix.

$$\vec{y}_n = A^n \cdot \vec{y}_0 \quad (10.30)$$

For a specific example, consider the following system of first order difference equations.

$$\begin{aligned} x_{n+1} &= x_n + y_n \\ y_{n+1} &= -2 \cdot x_n + 4 \cdot y_n \end{aligned} \quad (10.31)$$

This can be expressed in the following form:

$$\vec{y}_{n+1} = A \bullet \vec{y}_n \quad (10.32)$$

Powers for this particular matrix A were calculated in (10.28) and therefore the solution can be expressed as follows:

$$\begin{aligned} \begin{bmatrix} x_n \\ y_n \end{bmatrix} &= \begin{bmatrix} 2^{n+1} - 3^n & 3^n - 2^n \\ 2^{n+1} - 2 \cdot 3^n & 2 \cdot 3^n - 2^n \end{bmatrix} \bullet \begin{bmatrix} x_0 \\ y_0 \end{bmatrix} \\ &= \begin{bmatrix} x_0 \cdot (2^{n+1} - 3^n) + y_0 \cdot (3^n - 2^n) \\ x_0 \cdot (2^{n+1} - 2 \cdot 3^n) + y_0 \cdot (2 \cdot 3^n - 2^n) \end{bmatrix} \end{aligned} \quad (10.33)$$

Solving the Non-Homogenous First Order Linear System

Aside from treating the homogeneous system in (10.32) and (10.29), matrices can also be applied to a system that has additional term as shown below.

$$\vec{p}_{n+1} - A \cdot \vec{p}_n = \vec{f}_n \tag{10.34}$$

The easiest case for finding a particular solution is when $\vec{f}_n$ is a constant or simple function; in this case the particular solution can guessed. Once the particular solution is known, it is added to the homogeneous solution to get the final solution. The types of guesses that would most likely work are linear combinations of the guesses that would be used for a single equation in Table 9-3. The following example illustrates how to apply this technique.

$$\begin{bmatrix} x_{n+1} \\ y_{n+1} \end{bmatrix} - \begin{bmatrix} 1 & 1 \\ -2 & 4 \end{bmatrix} \cdot \begin{bmatrix} x_n \\ y_n \end{bmatrix} = \begin{bmatrix} 3^n \\ 3^n + n^2 \end{bmatrix} \tag{10.35}$$

Assume a particular solution of the form.

$$\vec{yp}_n = \begin{bmatrix} a_1 \cdot 3^n + b_1 \cdot n^2 + c_1 \cdot n + d_1 \\ a_2 \cdot 3^n + b_2 \cdot n^2 + c_2 \cdot n + d_2 \end{bmatrix} \tag{10.36}$$

Substituting (10.36) into (10.35) and introducing some new variables yields the following equation.

$$\begin{bmatrix} 3^n \cdot A + n^2 \cdot B + n \cdot C + D \\ 3^n \cdot E + n^2 \cdot F + n \cdot G + H_1 \end{bmatrix} = \begin{bmatrix} 3^n \\ 3^n + n^2 \end{bmatrix} \tag{10.37}$$

By equating all the 3^n, n^2, n, and constant terms, this leads to a system of 7 equations and 8 unknowns. Note that (10.38) and (10.42) are redundant.

$$A = 2 \cdot a_1 - a_2 = 1 \tag{10.38}$$
$$B = -b_2 = 0 \tag{10.39}$$
$$C = 2 \cdot b_1 - c_2 = 0 \tag{10.40}$$
$$D = b_1 + c_1 - d_2 = 0 \tag{10.41}$$
$$E = 2 \cdot a_1 - a_2 = 1 \tag{10.42}$$
$$F = 2 \cdot b_1 - 3 \cdot b_2 = 1 \tag{10.43}$$
$$G = 2 \cdot b_2 + 2 \cdot c_1 - 3 \cdot c_2 = 0 \tag{10.44}$$
$$H = b_2 + c_2 + 2 \cdot d_1 - 3 \cdot d_2 = 0 \tag{10.45}$$

Since there are less equations than unknowns, one can apply the additional constraint that $a_2 = 0$. Doing so yields the particular solution.

$$y p_n = \begin{bmatrix} \frac{1}{2} \cdot n^2 + \frac{3}{2} \cdot n + \frac{5}{2} \\ -3^n + n + 2 \end{bmatrix} \quad (10.46)$$

Combining (10.33) with (10.46) yields the total solution.

$$\begin{bmatrix} x_n \\ y_n \end{bmatrix} = \begin{bmatrix} c_0 \cdot (2^{n+1} - 3^n) + c_1 \cdot (3^n - 2^n) + \frac{1}{2} \cdot n^2 + \frac{3}{2} \cdot n + \frac{5}{2} \\ c_0 \cdot (2^{n+1} - 2 \cdot 3^n) + c_1 \cdot (2 \cdot 3^n - 2^n) - 3^n + n + 2 \end{bmatrix} \quad (10.47)$$

The constants c_0 and c_1 can be solved by applying the initial condition.

$$\begin{bmatrix} x_n \\ y_n \end{bmatrix}_{n=0} = \begin{bmatrix} x_0 \\ y_0 \end{bmatrix} = \begin{bmatrix} c_0 + \frac{5}{2} \\ c_1 + 1 \end{bmatrix}$$

$$\Rightarrow \begin{bmatrix} c_0 \\ c_1 \end{bmatrix} = \begin{bmatrix} x_0 - \frac{5}{2} \\ y_0 - 1 \end{bmatrix} \quad (10.48)$$

The final solution is therefore as follows.

$$\begin{bmatrix} x_n \\ y_n \end{bmatrix} = \begin{bmatrix} \left(x_0 - \frac{5}{2}\right) \cdot (2^{n+1} - 3^n) + (y_0 - 1) \cdot (3^n - 2^n) + \frac{1}{2} \cdot n^2 + \frac{3}{2} \cdot n + \frac{5}{2} \\ \left(x_0 - \frac{5}{2}\right) \cdot (2^{n+1} - 2 \cdot 3^n) + (y_0 - 1) \cdot (2 \cdot 3^n - 2^n) - 3^n + n + 2 \end{bmatrix} \quad (10.49)$$

Higher Order Systems of Equations vs. Higher Order Equations

In many cases, a higher order system of one variable can be replaced with a lower order system of two variables by introduction of a dummy variable. It is also sometimes possible to take a system of equations and decouple them into one variable. However, because a system of equations is typically harder to solve, the only time where this is really useful is when dealing with a system of equations of higher than first order. Consider the following system.

$$\begin{aligned} x_{n+2} + 3 \cdot x_{n+1} + x_n &= y_n \\ y_{n+1} - 2 \cdot y_n &= x_n \end{aligned} \quad (10.50)$$

Because this is higher than second order, this does not fit the format of the systems of equations that have been discussed so far. There are two approaches to solve this system. One approach is to decouple the system by eliminating the variable x_n and then solving that equation. A substitution of the second equation in to the first one yields:

$$y_{n+3} - 2 \cdot y_{n+2} + 3 \cdot y_{n+2} - 6 \cdot y_{n+1} + y_{n+1} - 2 \cdot y_n = y_n$$
$$\Rightarrow y_{n+3} + y_{n+2} - 5 \cdot y_{n+1} - 3 \cdot y_n = 0 \quad (10.51)$$

The above system can be solved. Once y_n is known, x_n can be found as well by substituting in the solution for y_n. So in this case, the number of variables can be reduced by accepting a higher order equation.

A second approach to solving (10.50) is to introduce a dummy variable.

$$z_n = x_{n+1} \quad (10.52)$$

Substituting this in yields the following system:

$$z_{n+1} + 3 \cdot z_n + x_n = y_n$$
$$y_{n+1} - 2 \cdot y_n = x_n \quad (10.53)$$
$$x_{n+1} = z_n$$

This system can be rearranged as follows:

$$\begin{bmatrix} x_{n+1} \\ y_{n+1} \\ z_{n+1} \end{bmatrix} = \begin{bmatrix} 0 & 0 & 1 \\ 1 & 2 & 0 \\ -1 & 1 & -3 \end{bmatrix} \bullet \begin{bmatrix} x_n \\ y_n \\ z_n \end{bmatrix} = 0 \quad (10.54)$$

Conclusion

This chapter has discussed systems of linear equations. One way of solving these systems is isolate one variable and substitute it into the other equations. Another approach is to express these systems using matrices and matrix algebra. It is a matter of personal preference which method to use and both equations will eventually lead to the correct solution.

Chapter 11

Other Topics in Difference Equations

Introduction

This chapter discusses the topics of equations with discontinuities, numerical methods, asymptotic behavior, and the Mandelbrot set.

Solving Equations with Discontinuities

Method of Breaking Up Equations

When equations have discontinuities, such as delta functions or step functions, it often leads to solutions that may also be discontinuous. One approach to solving equations of this kind is to break them up into multiple equations as done in the following example.

$$f_{n+1} + 3 \cdot f_n = \delta(n)$$
$$f_0 = 1$$
$$\delta(n) = \begin{cases} 1 & \text{for } n = 0 \\ 0 & \text{otherwise} \end{cases} \tag{11.1}$$

The first step in solving (11.1) is to solve for the case of **n = 0**.

$$f_1 + 3 \cdot f_0 = 1$$
$$\Rightarrow f_1 = -2 \tag{11.2}$$

The next step is to solve the case for **n > 0**, using the initial condition as found in (11.2)

$$f_n = \frac{2}{3} \cdot (-3)^n \tag{11.3}$$

Combining (11.2) and (11.3) yields the final solution.

$$f_n = \begin{cases} 1 & \text{for } n = 0 \\ \frac{2}{3} \cdot (-3)^n & \text{otherwise} \end{cases} \tag{11.4}$$

In this case, there was only one discontinuity, but this method could be expanded to any number of discontinuities.

Z Transform Method

The Z transform is discussed in much more depth in another chapter to follow, but can be thought of as the discrete analogy of the Laplace transform. Just as applying the Laplace transform can convert a differential equation to an algebraic equation, applying the Z transform can convert a difference equation to a similar result. For example, applying the Z transform to (11.1) yields an algebraic equation.

$$z \cdot F(z) - 1 \cdot z + 3 \cdot F(z) = 1 \tag{11.5}$$

$$F(z) = \frac{1+z}{z+3} = \frac{1}{z+3} + \frac{z}{z+3} \tag{11.6}$$

Taking the inverse Z transform of (11.6) yields the final solution, where $u(n-1)$ is a unit step function.

$$f_n = (-3)^{n-1} \cdot u(n-1) + (-3)^n \tag{11.7}$$

Numerical Methods

If the initial conditions are known, the numerical methods for difference equations are very powerful and easy to use. In fact, they are so straightforward and effective that there may be a temptation to resort to them immediately before even trying one of the previous methods that have been discussed. Using these methods may sacrifice some of the insights and satisfaction of finding the closed form solution, but there situations where numerical methods are the only option. To use this approach, the requirement is that the initial conditions need to be known. Once these initial conditions are known, then the higher order terms can be computed from these lower order terms. To illustrate this method, consider the following equation:

$$\begin{aligned} y_{n+2} - y_{n+1} - 0.5 \cdot (y_{n+1} - y_n)^2 &= 0 \\ y_0 &= 1 \\ y_1 &= 2 \end{aligned} \tag{11.8}$$

To solve this equation, express the highest order term in terms of the lower order terms.

$$y_{n+2} = y_{n+1} + 0.5 \cdot (y_{n+1} - y_{n+2})^2 \tag{11.9}$$

Starting out with the initial values of *1* and *2*, the other equations, the solution can be found.

N	y_n
0	1
1	2
2	2.5
3	2.625
4	2.632813
5	2.632843
6	2.632843
7	2.632843
8	2.632843
9	2.632843

Table 11-3 Solution to Equation (11.8)

Numerical methods are also effective in solving equations that involved discontinuities and complicated rules, like the following example.

Example

Consider a 50,000 liter heated pool of water that starts at 15°C which has a water fountain that outputs water at a rate of 1000 liters/minute. If the pool volume exceeds 50,000 liters, a drain becomes active to drain this water away. The fountain is sourced by two water tanks. One is the outdoor temperature of 15°C, and another is kept at 100°C. This fountain works in such a way to maintain the water at a comfortable temperature of 25°C. Every minute, there is a digital controller that monitors the temperature. If it is less than 24°C, then the fountain will use the hot water for the next minute. If it is more than 26°C, then the fountain will use the cold water. If it is between 24°C and 26°C, then no water is added. How long does it take the pool to warm up to a stable temperature?

When mixing water, the resulting temperature will be the weighted average of the temperatures. This can be expressed as a difference equation as:

$$t_{n+1} = \begin{cases} \dfrac{50 \cdot t_n + 100}{51} & \text{if } t_n < 24 \\ \dfrac{50 \cdot t_n + 15}{51} & \text{if } t_n > 26 \\ t_n & \text{if } 24 \leq t_n \leq 26 \end{cases} \quad (11.10)$$

Once the value at any time is known, it is easy to find it at the next time. The solution using numerical methods is in Table 11-4 and shows that after 6 minutes, a steady state temperature of 24.5°C is reached. This steady state temperature can change with initial conditions.

N	t_n
0	15
1	16.66667
2	18.30065
3	19.90260
4	21.47314
5	23.01288
6	24.52243
7	24.52243
8	24.52243
9	24.52243
10	24.52243

***Table 11-4**   Solution to Equation (11.10)*

Limiting (Asymptotic) Behavior

Sometimes one might be interested in the behavior of one or a set of difference equations as n approaches infinity. Even if the equations cannot be explicitly solved, there are methods that can still be used to find the limiting behavior. The most common types of limiting behaviors are that they could approach some limit, grow unbounded, or oscillate between two more values; all of these possibilities are discussed.

Difference Equations with a Solution that Approaches a Limit

Some difference equations have a solution that will tend to a limit as n approaches infinity. Proving that the solution actually does tend to a limit may be more difficult, but there is a simple method to find this limit if it exists. If the equation tends to a limit, then the following is true.

$$\lim_{n \to \infty}(y_n) = \lim_{n \to \infty}(y_{n+1}) = \ldots = \lim_{n \to \infty}(y_{n+k}) = y_\infty \qquad (11.11)$$

For example, consider the limiting behavior of the following equation.

$$y_{n+2} - y_{n+1} - 0.2 \cdot y_{n+1} \cdot (5 - y_{n+1}) + 0.1 \cdot (y_n)^2 = 0 \qquad (11.12)$$

After applying (11.11), we get equation (11.13) which has solution (11.14).

$$y_\infty - y_\infty - 0.2 \cdot y_\infty \cdot (5 - y_\infty) + 0.1 \cdot (y_\infty)^2 = 0 \qquad (11.13)$$

$$y_\infty = 0, \frac{10}{3} \qquad (11.14)$$

In this case, there are two solutions. For this equation, it turns out that the solution could tend to either of these limits or grow unbounded, depending on initial conditions. Table 11-5 shows initial conditions that could lead to all three of these conditions.

n	y_n
0	1.000
1	2.000
2	2.800
3	3.248
4	3.331
5	3.333
6	3.333
7	3.333
8	3.333
9	3.333
10	3.333

n	y_n
0	1
1	0
2	0
3	0
4	0
5	0
6	0
7	0
8	0
9	0
10	0

n	y_n
0	1
1	−1
2	−2.3
3	−6.187
4	−23.8577
5	−218.472
6	−14756
7	−6.5E+07
8	−1.3E+15
9	−4.9E+29
10	−7.3E+58

Table 11-5 *Limiting Behaviors for (11.12)*

Using Differences and Ratios to Better Understand Limiting Behavior of Solutions

In some cases, looking at the limiting behavior of the difference or ratio of the terms might give some insight to the conditions that are necessary the solution tends to a limit. Even in the cases that the solution does not tend to a limit, it can also give some insight as to what this nature of the behavior as in (11.15).

$$y_{n+2} = y_{n+1} + 0.5 \cdot (y_{n+1} - y_n)^2 \qquad (11.15)$$

To understand the limiting behavior of this equation, look at the difference of the terms.

$$\Delta y_{n+1} = 0.5 \cdot \Delta y_n^2 \qquad (11.16)$$

By solving (11.16) algebraically, we see that if difference of the terms approaches a limit, this limit would have to be *0* or *2*. Upon more careful analysis we find that Table 11-6 gives a good description of the limiting behavior.

Initial Conditions	Limiting Behavior	Solution
$\|y_1 - y_0\| < 2$	$\Delta y_n \to 0$	Tends to a limit.
$\|y_1 - y_0\| = 2$	$\Delta y_n \to 2$	Grows unbounded.
$\|y_1 - y_0\| > 2$	$\Delta y_n \to \infty$	Grows unbounded.

Table 11-6   Possible Outcomes of (11.15)

As another example for limiting behavior, consider the famous Fibonacci sequence.

$$1, 1, 2, 3, 5, 8, 13, 21, \ldots \qquad (11.17)$$

This sequence can be described by the following difference equation.

$$y_{n+2} = y_n + y_{n+1} \qquad (11.18)$$

If we assume that $y_{n+1}/y_n = r$, then we can substitute this into (11.18) to see that the ratio of the terms does approach a limit.

$$r = \frac{1}{r} + 1$$
$$\Rightarrow r = \frac{1+\sqrt{5}}{2} \qquad (11.19)$$

Although there were actually two roots in the equation, we could rule out the negative root because the sequence has no negative terms. This number actually has a special name in mathematics – *the golden mean*.

Fractal Geometry – The Mandelbrot Set

Difference equations can be used to generate fractals, such as the *Mandelbrot Set*. To do this, we first start with equation (11.20) with a zero initial condition and consider the values for the parameter *c* that lead to a solution that is bounded as *n* approaches infinity.

$$y_{n+1} = y_n^2 + c \qquad (11.20)$$

In this equation, y_n and *c* can be complex numbers. The value of *c* is plotted in the complex plane by expressing the coordinates in the form $i \cdot x + i \cdot y$. Figure 11-1 was generated by plotting the blue points if the value was less than 500 iterations after 1000 iterations and purple points if the value was less than 5 after 10 iterations. The code to generate these plots is much simpler than one might think and is in the appendix.

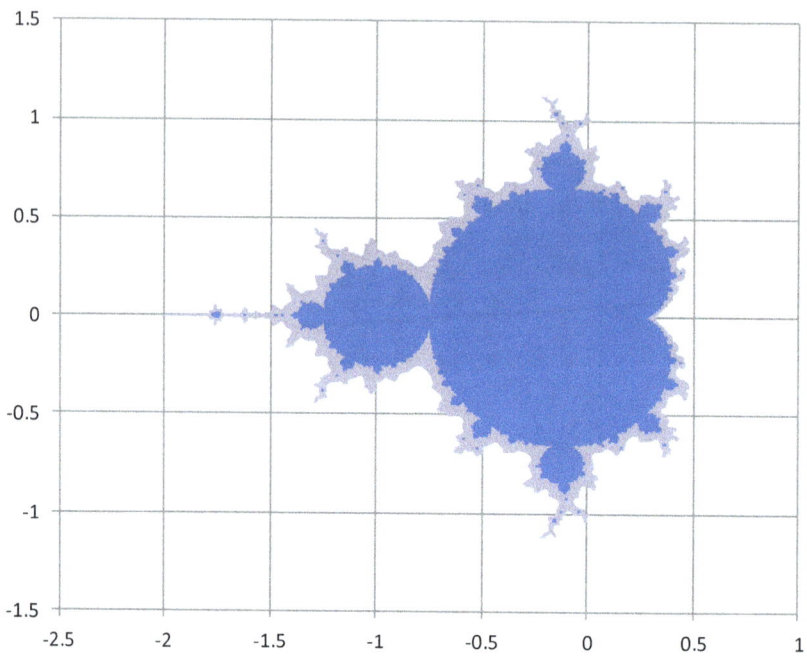

Figure 11-1   *The Mandelbrot Set*

Conclusion

For some difference equations, numerical methods may be the only way to solve them. It turns out that numerical methods are very simple to do if the initial conditions are known. These methods can be applied quite easily to equations with discontinuities, strange rules, or even systems of equations.

In some situations, the limiting behavior of difference equations is of interest. It may be possible to solve for the limiting values of equations even if there is not a general closed form solution. Limiting behavior also leads into fractal geometry, for which some plots can be generated based on which initial conditions lead to a bounded solution.

Appendix
Excel VBA Code for Generation of Mandelbrot Set

```
Sub GenerateMandelbrot_Click()
Dim Xmin As Double, Xmax As Double, Ymin As Double, Ymax As Double, Increment As Double
Dim x As Double, y As Double, Zr As Double, Zi As Double, z as Double
Dim iYmax As Integer, iXmax As Integer, Row as Integer, MaxOrbits As Long, OrbitTol As Double
Dim iX As Integer, iY As Integer, LastInSet As Boolean, InSet As Boolean
    Xmin = -0.2
    Xmax = 0.5
    Ymin = -1.2
    Ymax = 1.2
    Increment = 0.4
    MaxOrbits = 10
    OrbitTol = 5
    Row = 10
    iXmax = (Xmax - Xmin) / Increment
    iYmax = (Ymax - Ymin) / Increment
    For iY = 0 To iYmax
       y = Ymin + iY * Increment
       LastInSet = False
       For iX = 0 To iXmax
          x = Xmin + iX * Increment
          Zr = 0
          Zi = 0
          InSet = True
          For i = 1 To MaxOrbits
             z = Zr
             Zr = 2 * Zr ^ 2 - 2 * Zi ^ 2 + x
             Zi = 4 * z * Zi + y
             If Zr ^ 2 + Zi ^ 2 > OrbitTol Then
                InSet = False
                Exit For
             End If
          Next i
          If InSet = True Then
             Cells(Row, 1) = x
             Cells(Row, 2) = y
             Row = Row + 1
          End If
       Next iX
    Next iY
End
```

From Analog Electronics to Digital Electronics

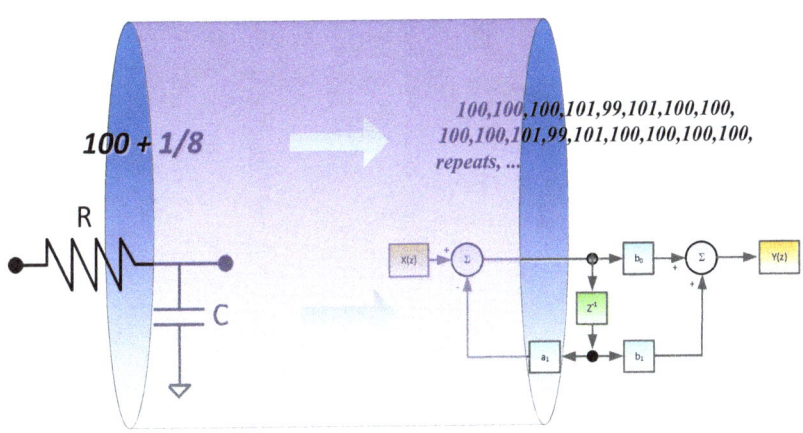

Chapter 12

The Discrete Z Transform

Introduction

The Laplace transform is a very powerful tool used to solve many problems ranging from differential equations, circuit analysis, and filter responses. The Z transform is the discrete equivalent of the Laplace transform.

Derivation of Z Transform from Laplace Transform

The Laplace transform is defined as follows:

$$F(s) = \int_0^\infty f(t) \cdot e^{-st} \cdot dt \qquad (12.1)$$

In equation (12.1), the variable *t* can be thought of as time. If time is sampled at discrete intervals, then *t* can be expressed in terms of the time increment, **T**.

$$t = n \cdot T \qquad (12.2)$$

Assuming that the time increment is small, then the integral of the Laplace transform can be approximated with a *Riemann sum*.

$$F(s) = \lim_{T \to 0} \left[\sum_{n=0}^\infty f(n \cdot T) \cdot e^{-nsT} \cdot T \right]$$
$$\approx \sum_{n=0}^\infty f(n \cdot T) \cdot e^{-n \cdot s \cdot T} \cdot T \qquad (12.3)$$

In order to express (12.3) in terms that are used with the Z transform, the new variable *z* is defined and new function *g(n)* is defined.

$$z = e^{s \cdot T} \qquad (12.4)$$
$$g(n) = f(n \cdot T) \qquad (12.5)$$

Making these substitutions into (12.3) gives the formal definition of Z transform:

$$G(z) = \sum_{n=0}^\infty g(n) \cdot z^{-n} \qquad (12.6)$$

Because (12.6) was derived from (12.3), this implies that as the sampling period approaches zero, Z transform becomes the Laplace Transform.

Similarities Between the Z and Laplace Transforms

The Laplace and Z transform are related in their definition and as a result, they have some similar properties. Table 12-3 shows some of the commonly used properties of Laplace and Z transforms.

Property	Continuous Time Laplace Domain		Discrete Time Z Domain	
Linearity	$a \cdot f(t) + b \cdot g(t)$	$a \cdot F(s) + b \cdot G(s)$	$a \cdot f(n) + b \cdot g(n)$	$a \cdot F(z) + b \cdot G(z)$
Time Shifting	$f(t-\tau)$	$e^{s \cdot \tau} F(s)$	$f(n-k)$	$z^{-k} \cdot F(z)$
Derivative/ Difference	$f'(t)$	$s \cdot F(s)$	$f(n) - f(n-1)$	$(1 - z^{-1}) \cdot Y(z)$
Integral/ Sum	$\int f(t)$	$\frac{1}{s} \cdot F(s)$	$\sum f(n)$	$\frac{1}{1 - z^{-1}} \cdot F(z)$
Ramp	$t \cdot f(t)$	$-\frac{d}{ds} F(s)$	$n \cdot f(n)$	$-z \cdot \frac{d}{dz} F(z)$
Final Value Theorems	$f(0) = \lim_{s \to \infty}(s \cdot F(s))$ $f(\infty) = \lim_{s \to 0}(s \cdot F(s))$		$f(0) = \lim_{z \to \infty}(F(z))$ $f(\infty) = \lim_{z \to 1}((1 - z^{-1}) \cdot F(s))$	

Table 12-3 Comparing Laplace and Z Transforms

For the Z transform, a widely used relationship that is useful to become familiar with is the time shifting property which is that multiplying by z^{-1} is the equivalent to a one clock cycle delay in the time domain. Recall that in Laplace domain, multiplying by the variable s is related to taking a derivative and that multiplying by $1 - z^{-1}$ is in the Z domain is related to taking a finite difference. Many of the properties in Table 12-3 show this relationship, although one should be cautious as there are also plenty of exceptions to this pattern as well. The following example illustrates further the similarities.

Example
Find the Laplace transform of $f(t) = t$ and the Z transform of $f(n) = n$.

The Laplace transform can be calculated as follows:

$$F(s) = \int_0^\infty t \cdot e^{-s \cdot t} \, dt = -\frac{t^2}{2} \cdot \frac{e^{-s \cdot t}}{s} \bigg|_0^\infty - \int_0^\infty \frac{e^{-s \cdot t}}{s} \, dt = \frac{1}{s^2} \quad (12.7)$$

The Z transform is calculated in (12.8).

$$F(z) = \sum_{n=0}^{\infty} n \cdot z^{-n} \qquad (12.8)$$

This summation was found by relating it to the derivative of a geometric series.

$$\begin{aligned} F(z) &= \sum_{n=0}^{\infty} n \cdot z^{-n} \\ &= -z \cdot \frac{d}{dz}\left(\sum_{n=0}^{\infty} z^{-n}\right) = z \cdot \frac{d}{dz}\left(\frac{z}{1-z}\right) = \frac{z}{(z-1)^2} \end{aligned} \qquad (12.9)$$

Comparing (12.7) and (12.9), the Z transform often looks like the Laplace transform with s replaced with the expression $1 - z^{-1}$, with the z in the numerator representing a shift of one clock cycle. Table 12-4 shows many other Laplace and Z transforms.

Continuous Time		Discrete Time	
Function	Laplace Transform	Function	Z Transform
$\delta(t-k)$	1	$\delta(n-k)$	z^{-k}
$u(t)$	$\dfrac{1}{s}$	$u(n)$	$\dfrac{z}{z-1}$
$u(t-k)$	e^{-sk}	$u(n-k)$	$z^{-k}\dfrac{z}{z-1}$
$t \cdot u(t)$	$\dfrac{1}{s^2}$	$n \cdot u(n)$	$\dfrac{z}{(z-1)^2}$
$t^2 \cdot u(t)$	$\dfrac{2}{s^3}$	$n^2 \cdot u(n)$	$\dfrac{z \cdot (z+1)}{(z-1)^3}$
$a^t \cdot u(t)$	$\dfrac{1}{s - \ln|a|}$	$a^n \cdot u(t)$	$\dfrac{z}{z-a}$

Table 12-4 *Laplace and Z Transform Pairs*

In the table, note the unit step function, **u(t)**, multiplies all the time domain responses. The discrete time analogy to this function is **u(n)**, which is given in (12.10).

$$u(n) = \begin{cases} 0 & \text{for } n < 0 \\ 1 & \text{otherwise} \end{cases} \qquad (12.10)$$

In most cases, multiplying each time domain function by *u(n)* is unnecessary, because both the Laplace and Z transforms are defined for *n*>0. However, there are some situations where it is important to keep this factor, such as when the index gets shifted.

The other function introduced in Table 12-4 is the discrete delta function, *δ(t)*, which is defined in (12.11). In the continuous time domain, this function is zero everywhere except *t*=0 and at this point has infinite value such that the integral of this function is equal to one. The discrete analogy of this function is very similar.

$$\delta(n) = \begin{cases} 1 & \text{for } n = 0 \\ 0 & \text{otherwise} \end{cases} \quad (12.11)$$

Solving Difference Equations with the Z Transform

The time shifting property enables one to translate a shift in the time index to a multiple of the variable *z*. Table 12-5 shows this property as well as the impact of the initial conditions.

Function	Z Transform	Justification
$f(n+1)$	$z \cdot F(z) - z \cdot f(0)$	$\sum_{n=0}^{\infty} f(n+1) \cdot z^{-n} = z \cdot \sum_{j=1}^{\infty} f(j) \cdot z^{-j}$ $= z \cdot \left[\left(\sum_{j=0}^{\infty} f(j) \cdot z^{-j} \right) - f(0) \right]$ $z \cdot F(z) - z \cdot f(0)$
$f(n+2)$	$z^2 \cdot F(z) - z^2 \cdot f(1) - z \cdot f(0)$	$Z\{f(n+2)\} = Z\{f(n+1)+1)\}$ $= z \cdot Z\{f(n+1)\} - z \cdot f(0)$ $= z^2 \cdot F(z) - z^2 \cdot f(1) - z \cdot f(0)$
$f(n+k)$	$z^k \cdot F(z) - z^k \cdot f(k-1)$ $- \sum_{i=0}^{k-1} z^{-i} \cdot f(i)$	Use similar reasoning as above

Table 12-5   *Time Shifting in and the Z Domain*

It therefore follows that if the Z transform is applied to a linear difference equation, then it can be transformed into an algebraic equation in the Z domain. If this algebraic equation can be rearranged to have the unknown function on one side of the equation and an expression with a known inverse Z transform on the other side, then the solution can be found. This method often is a good one to try to difference equations involving discontinuous functions, such as the step function and delta function.

For example, consider solving the following example using the Z transform.

$$f_{n+1} + 3 \cdot f_n = \delta(n)$$
$$f_0 = 1 \qquad (12.12)$$

Applying the rules in Table 12-5 yields an algebraic equation.

$$z \cdot F(z) - 1 \cdot z + 3 \cdot F(z) = 1 \qquad (12.13)$$

$$F(z) = \frac{1+z}{z+3} = \frac{1}{z+3} + \frac{z}{z+3} \qquad (12.14)$$

Looking up these functions in Table 12-4 allows the solution can be found as:

$$f_n = (-3)^{n-1} \cdot u(n-1) + (-3)^n \qquad (12.15)$$

Calculating the Frequency Response from the Z Domain

Just as the Laplace transform can be used to find the frequency response for analog circuits, the Z transform can be used in a similar way to find the frequency response for digital circuits such as digital filters and delta sigma modulators. For the Laplace transform in the s domain, the frequency response can be found by substituting $j \cdot \omega \rightarrow s$, where $j = \sqrt{-1}$. After this substitution is done, the magnitude of the complex function will be the frequency response. The approach is very similar in the Z domain and is done with the substitution (12.16), where T is the sampling period.

$$e^{j \cdot \omega \cdot T} \rightarrow z \qquad (12.16)$$

A simplifying approach is just to express the frequency, ω, in terms of the sampling period, so this makes $T = 1$ and simplifies the substitution to something slightly simpler.

$$e^{j \cdot \omega} \rightarrow z \qquad (12.17)$$

Euler's identity often is necessary to calculate the frequency response and is given as follows.

$$e^{j \cdot \omega} = \cos(\omega) + j \cdot \sin(\omega) \qquad (12.18)$$

Example:
Calculate the frequency response of a digital circuit with the following transfer function:

$$F(z) = \frac{1}{z+1} \tag{12.19}$$

The frequency response can be obtained by applying (12.16) to (12.19). For this, the frequency is normalized to the sampling frequency, *1/T*.

$$f(\omega) = |F(e^{j\omega})| = \left|\frac{1}{e^{j\omega}+1}\right| = \frac{1}{|\cos(\omega)+j\cdot\sin(\omega)+1|}$$
$$= \frac{1}{\sqrt{(\cos(\omega)+1)^2 + \sin^2(\omega)}} = \frac{1}{\sqrt{2+2\cdot\cos(\omega)}} \tag{12.20}$$

Determining Stability in the Z Domain

General Criteria

Recall that in the analog domain, the requirement for stability is that all the poles are in the left hand plane. The implications for this in the digital domain can be found by combining result (12.4) and Euler's identity.

$$z = e^s = e^{real(s)+j\cdot imag(s)}$$
$$\Rightarrow |z_{pole}| = e^{real(s_{pole})} \tag{12.21}$$
$$|z_{pole}| < 1 \Leftrightarrow real(s_{pole}) < 0$$

So for a digital system to be stable, the poles must satisfy the following.

$$|z_{pole}| < 1 \tag{12.22}$$

Example
Determine the stability of the following system with the following transfer function.

$$G(z) = \frac{1}{(z-0.7)\cdot(z^2 + 1/4)} \tag{12.23}$$

The poles of this system are at **0.7** and **± 0.5·i**. Since all of these have a magnitude less than one, the system is stable.

Jury's Stability Test

Recall that *Routh's Stability Criteria* is a useful rule for analog transfer functions to determine if the poles all have negative real parts without requiring the roots of the denominator to be calculated. *Jury's Test* is a similar test for digital transfer functions that can be applied to a polynomial to determine if all the roots have magnitude less than one. To use this test, first divide through by the highest order term and express the polynomial as follows:

$$Q(z) = z^n + a_{n-1} \cdot z^{n-1} + \ldots + a_0 \qquad (12.24)$$

The roots of $Q(z)$ will have roots with magnitude of less than one, thus implying stability of the system, if and only if the following criteria are met.

$$Q(1) > 0 \qquad (12.25)$$
$$(-1)^n \cdot Q(-1) > 0 \qquad (12.26)$$
$$|a_0| < 1 \qquad (12.27)$$
$$|b_0| > |b_{n-1}|, |c_0| > |c_{n-2}|, \ldots \qquad (12.28)$$

To determine the coefficients for criteria (12.28), a jury matrix needs to be constructed as shown in Table 12-6.

z^0	z^1	...	z^i	...	z^{n-1}	z^n
a_0	a_1	...	a_i	...	a_{n-1}	1
1	a_{n-1}	...	a_{n-i}	...	a_1	a_0
b_0	b_1	...	b_i	...	b_{n-1}	0
b_{n-1}	b_{n-2}	...	b_{n-1-i}	...	b_0	0
c_0	c_1	...	c_i	...	0	0
c_{n-2}	c_{n-3}	...	c_{n-2-i}	...	0	0
...	...	...	...	...	...	...

Table 12-6 Jury Matrix

The first row is formed by listing all the coefficients and the second row is just these coefficients reversed. The coefficients for the third row are found by taking the following determinant.

$$b_i = \begin{vmatrix} a_0 & a_{n-i} \\ 1 & a_i \end{vmatrix} = a_0 \cdot a_i - a_{n-i} \qquad (12.29)$$

The fourth row is just the third row reversed. The fifth row is found in a similar row as the third row as follows. This process continues for more rows.

$$c_i = \begin{vmatrix} b_0 & b_{n-i-1} \\ b_{n-1} & b_i \end{vmatrix} \qquad (12.30)$$

Example
Determine if a system with the following transfer function is stable.

$$\frac{Output}{Input} = T(z) = \frac{1+3 \cdot z}{0.25 - z + z^2 - 4 \cdot z^3} \quad (12.31)$$

The polynomial used to determine stability is as follows:

$$Q(z) = z^3 - 0.25 \cdot z^2 + 0.25 \cdot z - 0.0625 \quad (12.32)$$

It turns out that the roots of this polynomial are at 0.25 and $\pm 0.5i$. Suppose we did not know this and let us use Jury's stability criteria. The Jury matrix for this system is shown below.

	z^0	z^1	z^2	z^3
a_0	−0.0625	0.2500	−0.2500	1
a_3	1	−0.2500	0.2500	−0.0625
b_0	−0.9961	0.2344	−0.2344	0
b_2	−0.2344	0.2344	−0.9961	0
c_0	0.9373	−0.1785	0	0
c_1	−0.1785	0.9373	0	0

Table 12-7   Jury Matrix

The system is stable because all of the stability criteria as stated in Table 12-8 are satisfied.

Statement	Evaluation	Verdict
$Q(1) > 0$	$0.9375 > 0$	Satisfied
$(-1)^3 \cdot Q(-1) > 0$	$1.5625 > 0$	Satisfied
$|a_0| < 1$	$|-0.0625| < 1$	Satisfied
$|b_0| > |b_{n-1}|$	$|-0.9961| > |-0.2344|$	Satisfied
$|c_0| > |c_{n-2}|$	$|0.9373| > |-0.1785|$	Satisfied

Table 12-8   Jury Test Example

Conclusion

The Z transform is a powerful tool that can be used to solve difference equations and analyze digital systems in terms of frequency response and stability.

Chapter 13

Converting Between Analog and Digital Signals

Introduction

The advantage of converting a time-varying analog signal into a stream of discrete numbers is that it allows a vast range of digital processing. Although this analog signal does not necessarily have to be a voltage, there is no loss of generality for the concepts presented in this chapter in thinking of it in this way. The common electronic component that converts a time-varying voltage to a stream of numbers is the *Analog to Digital Converter*, or better known as ADC. Two key concepts for the analog to digital conversion process are *quantization* and *sampling*. Quantization is the process of approximating with the nearest value, such as rounding a measured voltage to the nearest 0.01 volt. *Sampling* refers to making measurements at periodic increments of time. This chapter discusses these concepts and others involved in converting between analog and digital signals.

Quantization

Process of Quantization

The process of quantization involves rounding a measured value to some closest discrete value. This is typically done by an N-bit *quantizer* that has 2^N levels that are evenly spaced apart. For example, a 5-bit analog to digital converter is an example of a quantizer that accepts an input voltage of 0 to 4 volts would round to the nearest 0.25 volt and the maximum potential error in this conversion process would be 0.125 volts, which corresponds to ½ bit.

For analog to digital converters, it is always desirable to have finer resolution and faster speed, but this comes at the expense of other factors, such as cost and current consumption. For this reason, if the amplitude of the input signal is less than what the ADC can handle, a *variable gain amplifier* can be used to match these levels up to ensure that one gets the maximum best performance out of the ADC.

Quantization Noise - Signal to Noise Ratio of an ADC

The result derived in this section is a variation of the result as derived in reference [3]. This widely used result pertains to the *signal to noise ratio* of an analog to digital converter sampling a sine wave. This is a reasonable assumption because any periodic signal can be thought of as a sum of sinusoidal waveforms. To derive the result, it is assumed that the full amplitude of the ADC is being used and the signal of interest is of the form:

$$v(t) = \frac{2^N}{2} \cdot \sin(f \cdot t) \qquad (13.1)$$

The *root mean square* (RMS) voltage is used because this voltage is not constant. The RMS value of the signal in (13.1) is given as follows.

$$\sqrt{\int_0^{2\pi/f} \left(\frac{2^N}{2} \cdot \sin(f \cdot t)\right)^2 \cdot dt} = \frac{2^{N-1}}{\sqrt{2}} \tag{13.2}$$

The *quantization noise* is the voltage error due to rounding off the signal to the nearest bit and can be treated as a uniformly distributed random variable that varies between 0 and ½ over one sampling period. The RMS value of this noise is given in (13.3).

$$\sqrt{\int_0^1 \left(t - \frac{1}{2}\right)^2 \cdot dt} = \frac{1}{\sqrt{12}} \tag{13.3}$$

The signal to noise ratio is defined as the power of the signal to the power of the noise. Because power is related to the square of the voltage, this quantity can be calculated by dividing (13.2) by (13.3) and then squaring this amount. Signal to noise ratio is typically expressed in decibels, which means to take the log of the value and multiply by 10. Doing all these operations yields the result in (13.4) which is also the result derived in [3].

$$\begin{aligned}\frac{S}{N} &= 10 \cdot \log\left(\frac{2^{N-1}/\sqrt{2}}{\left(\frac{1}{\sqrt{12}}\right)}\right)^2 \\ &= 20 \cdot \log\left(\frac{\sqrt{6}}{2}\right) + 20 \cdot \log(2) \cdot N \\ &\approx 1.76 + 6.02 \cdot N\end{aligned} \tag{13.4}$$

Sampling

Sampling Rate

There are many situations where it might make sense to sample a signal at discrete moments of time. This could be monitoring the closing price of a stock each day, sampling a waveform representing a speech or communications signal, or a vast host of other situations. If the signal is not changing with time, then a single measurement would be sufficient to describe the signal for all time, but periodic sampling of the signal is necessary for signals that change over time. If we denote the time between each sample as *T* and the sampling frequency as f_s, then they can be related by equation (13.5).

$$T = \frac{1}{f_s} \tag{13.5}$$

Table 13-3 gives some sampling rates and common frequencies for some various situations.

Phenomenon	Frequency	Related Sampling Applications	(f_s)
Human Eye [1]	60 Hz	Computer Screen Refresh Rate	60 Hz
		Movie Picture Frame Rate	24 Hz
Human Speech	4 kHz	Digital voice sampling rate	8 kHz
Maximum Human Hearing	20 kHz	Compact Disk	44 kHz
		Digital Sound for Films	48 kHz

Table 13-3 *Some Typical Sampling Frequencies*

Aliasing Effects Due to Insufficient Sampling Rate

Aliasing is an undesired phenomenon where two signals of different frequencies can have the same samples. A good example to illustrate this is to consider a spinning wheel in Figure 13-1 where the position of the wheel is observed at times t_0 and t_2 are shown. Based on just these two observations, it would be unclear whether the wheel was spinning clockwise or counterclockwise at one third of the rate. However, if an observation was made at time t_1, then it would be more clear which way the wheel was rotating.

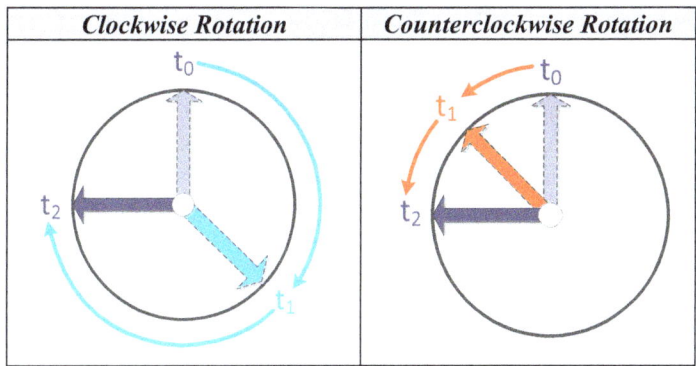

Figure 13-1 *Aliasing Example*

Reference [1] describes the phenomenon called the wagon wheel effect where a rapidly spinning wheel appears to be spinning in the opposite direction than it actually is. The explanation offered is that the human eye samples at a rate of approximately 60 frames/second and interprets as the slower rotating case when there is an ambiguity. For instance, if an object is spinning at a clockwise rate of 75 revolutions/second and the human eye observes this at a rate of 60 samples/second, then it will likely appear as 15 revolutions/second counterclockwise.

Expanding this principle in more general terms, if the frequency being sampled is f, then the alias frequency will be the difference between this frequency and the closest integer multiple of the sample rate. For example, if one samples a 378 MHz signal at 100 MHz, the alias frequency is 22 MHz. In cases where the sampled signal has unwanted higher frequency noise, an *anti-aliasing filter* can be used to ensure that this noise above the bandwidth of the intended signal does not get aliased down to frequencies that can be interpreted as the intended signal.

The Nyquist Criterion for Minimum Sample Rate and Oversampling

It has been shown that sampling too slow can cause aliasing effects. This begs the question of how fast of a sample rate is necessary to avoid aliasing. The *Nyquist Criteria* states that if a signal is sampled at a rate of at least twice the highest frequency component that it has, then aliasing effects can be avoided. By doing this, the alias frequency is shifted higher than the rate of the sampled signal, which effectively eliminates the problem of aliasing. Relating back to the spinning wheel example in Figure 13-1, consider this spinning at a rate of one revolution per second in the clockwise direction. If it was to start at the 12:00 position and was measured once per second, all my samples would be in the 12:00 position and it would appear the wheel was not spinning at all. If it was sampled at the Nyquist rate of two samples per second, there would be alternating samples at 12:00 and 6:00 positions. From these samples, one could correctly determine the wheel was spinning at one revolution per second, although it would be unclear if it was spinning in the clockwise or counterclockwise direction. If the sample rate was more than twice per second, then both the speed and direction of the wheel turning could be correctly determined. This is also related to why many of the sampling rates in Table 13-3 are about twice the frequency of the phenomenon being sampled.

Sampling faster than the Nyquist rate is known as *oversampling*. This has the benefits of pushing the alias frequency to higher frequencies so that it can be filtered easier which eases the requirements on the anti-aliasing filter. This technique is used in certain kinds of A/D converters for improved performance.

Delta Sigma ADC Converters

The delta sigma ADC converter takes oversampling to the extreme by only using a single bit (2-state) input with a high sample rate and is shown in Figure 13-2. The concept is that although the resolution is low, the high sample rate spreads the noise energy out over a wide range where it is easier to filter out the alias image. Once filtered, this single bit output is then run through a *decimation filter* which reduces the sample rate by N but in turn changes the output from 1 bit to N bits. Then it can be filtered to achieve a good signal to noise ratio. The Digital to Analog Converter (DAC) is used with the integrator to add the accumulated error to the input.

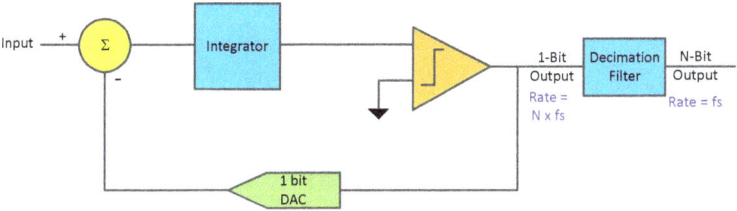

Figure 13-2   *Delta Sigma A/D Converter*

Figure 13-3 illustrates the concept of oversampling used in A/D converters. The total noise power for the case of both oversampling and no oversampling is the same, but the oversampled signal spreads the noise out over higher frequencies, where it is easier to filter. In this case, if there was a brick wall filter with bandwidth $0.5 \cdot f_s$, then only one-fourth of the noise of the oversampled signal would pass through the filter. Reducing the noise power by a factor of 4, is the equivalent of reducing the noise voltage by a factor of two, which is in turn equivalent to 1 bit improvement in the ADC resolution.

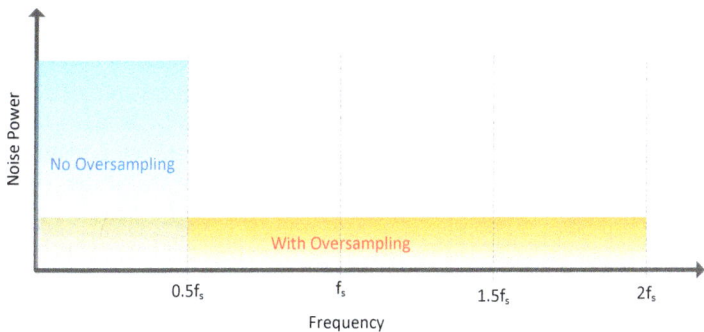

Figure 13-3   *Noise Spectrum of Oversampled Signal*

Digital to Analog Conversion

The reverse of analog to digital conversion is digital to analog conversion. Many of the concepts that apply ADC converters, such as sampling rate, Nyquist criterion, and signal to noise ratio also apply to digital to analog converters (DAC). Because the DAC will generate quantization noise of its own, it typically needs a *filter* to smooth it out. The bandwidth of this filter needs to be wide enough to allow the desired lower frequency components of the signal out, but not too wide as to let too much quantization noise get to the output.

The output of a DAC is assumed to be a voltage, but these same concepts can also be generalized to cover other cases, such as a temperature, divide value, or on/off state as discussed in the following sections.

Pulse Width Modulation

Pulse width modulation is a special case of digital to analog conversion where there are only two states, on and off. The duration of the on and off times are adjusted in order to make the average value equal to the desired value. In some cases, it might be necessary to place a filter after the output, but in other cases the object that this modulated signal is presented to naturally averages (filters) the input and the filter is not necessary.

Two State On/Off Control Systems

Two state on/off control systems have only the states of on and off and use pulse width modulation while also monitoring the output. A good example of this is a heating system, although the concept that can be generalized to other types of applications. If the temperature is below the thermostat temperature, the thermostat turns the heater on, otherwise the heater is off. For this system to work, we have to assume that the maximum achievable temperature is at or above the ambient outdoor temperature. For example, suppose the outside temperature is 50°C, the desired temperature is 70°C, and if one was to leave the heater on all the time, the temperature would eventually settle to 90°C. If the ambient outdoor temperature and starting room temperature were at 50°C, then the heater would stay on until it reaches 70°C. This system would not be able to achieve any temperatures above 90°C or below 50°C.

In general, the heating system is an example of a *bang bang control system*, where the system has only two states it can alternate between. This kind of system is fairly simple, but sometimes there are considerations when the system gets close to the target value. For instance, if the target temperature for the heating system is 70°C, then it might not be desirable for the heater to come on when the temperature fell below 69.999°C and turn off when it went above 70.001°C, which would result in *oscillation*. For a heating system, this would probably make some annoying noise and wear out the system faster.

Fortunately, there are approaches to prevent this. One approach to eliminating oscillation is *hysteresis*. This concept involves choosing different thresholds for the system to turn on and turn off. In this example, the heater might turn on when the temperature falls below 68°C and turn off when the temperature goes above 72°C. Another approach might be to establish a minimum on time. In the example of the heating system, perhaps it would come on for a minimum of 5 minutes before it turned off.

Although this example is for a heating system, this same concept can be applied to many other systems. Another application might be a systems work to maintain a voltage by having the ability to source current into a capacitor to raise the voltage. When the system is off, there is a resistor or some leakage path that decreases the voltage.

Three State Systems

Some systems have three states, positive, off, and negative. For example, the heating system could be expanded to have three states of heat, off, and cool. In this case, when the system reaches the target temperature, oscillation is probably more of a concern because it would be inefficient to have a system always turning on the heating and cooling. For this situation, hysteresis or a minimum on time is a must.

A voltage regulator is another example of a three state system. It works to produce an accurate output voltage that is different from the input. One common approach to this is to monitor the output voltage and compare to a reference voltage. If this is clearly too high, then the regulator sinks current to reduce the voltage. If the output voltage is clearly too low, then the regulator sources current to increase the output voltage. However, if the output voltage is within some tolerance of the target voltage called the *dead band*, then no corrections are made. The end result of doing this is producing a regulator that gives a cleaner, lower noise output.

Another such example of a three state system is the charge pump / phase detector of a phased locked loop as described in [5]. This works by most of the time having no corrections. At periodic instances in time, the circuit comes on to either deliver a positive or negative correction that is proportional to the input. In general this works well except when the desired correction becomes smaller than it is practical to implement with electronic components. This area is known as the *dead zone* of the phase detector. In this case, the phase detector resolves this problem by having a minimum correction to avoid this problem when the input is close to zero. In other digital feedback systems, sometimes there is a problem where the input is very close to zero. Some approaches to this are to always add some small error to the signal, or establish a minimum correction pulse width.

Delta Sigma Modulation

Delta sigma modulation is a form of digital to analog conversion that involves intentionally switching between two or more states in a rapid manner in such a way that much of the desired noise is pushed to higher frequencies. Single bit modulation involves switching between just two states. This is the case for pulse width modulation and also some DAC converters. Multi-bit modulation is the case when there are more than two states. An Nth order modulator will have 2^N states. For instance, to produce a value of 3/8, the following table shows the sequence of numbers that can be traversed through such that the average value is 3/8. In general, the higher order modulator will push out this undesired noise to higher frequencies, where it can be filtered better.

Modulator Order	Sequence
First	0, 0, 0, 0, 0, 0, 0, 1, … (repeats)
Second	0, 0, 0, 1, −1 ,1 ,0 ,0 ,0 ,0 ,1 ,− 1, 1, 0, 0, 0, … (repeats)
Third	0, 0, 1, −1 ,1 ,0 ,−1, 2, −2, 2, −1, 1, −1, 2, −2, 1, … (repeats)
Fourth	0, 0, 1, 0, −2, 3, −1, −1, 1, 2, −3, 1, 2, −2, 1, 0, 0, 1, −2, 2, 1, −3, 2, 1, −1, −1, 3, −2, 0, 1, 0, 0 …(repeats)

Table 13-4   *Delta Sigma Modulation Sequence for 1/8*

By calculating the *Fourier series* of the above sequence, the following spectral plot can be generated as shown in Figure 13-4. The noise generated by these sequences will be in the form of *spurs*, which is noise concentrated at discrete frequencies. Figure 13-4 shows the spectrum of the various modulator orders and shows that the higher order modulators have lower close-in spurious noise that come at the expense of more spurious noise at higher frequencies. By pushing the spurious noise to higher frequencies, it is easier to filter this out with a low pass filter.

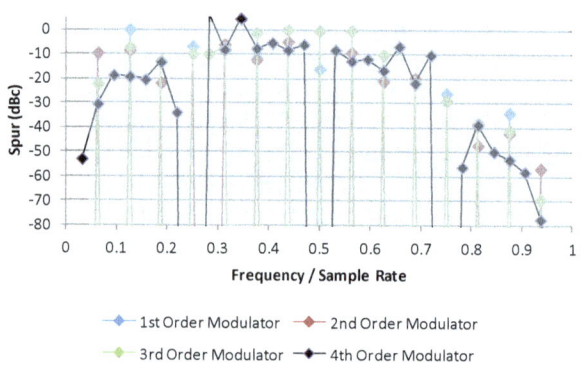

Figure 13-4   *Spectrum of Delta Sigma Sequence*

Delta Sigma Modulation and Fractional Frequency Dividers

The fractional frequency divider is a device that can take an input frequency and divide it by a fraction. It is easy to make a divider to divide by an integer such as 100 or 101, but more effort is required to create a divider to divide by a fractional value. Fractional dividers use delta sigma modulation by alternating the divider value between two frequencies. For instance, if one wanted to produce a fractional divide value of 100.125 with a second order modulator, Table 13-4 would imply a divide sequence as follows:

$$100, 100, 100, 101, 99, 101, 100, 100, 100, 100, 101, 99, 101, 100, 100, 100, 100, repeats, \ldots \quad (13.6)$$

In general, if the spur energy is viewed as quantization noise, $Q(z)$, then the noise shaping for the nth order delta sigma modulator will be [2]:

$$Y(z) = x(z) + (1 - z^{-1})^n \cdot Q(z) \qquad (13.7)$$

The sequence shown in (13.6) is relatively simple, but for larger fractions this sequence can get much more complicated. With a process called *dithering*, the numbers in the sequence can be mixed up, which has the impact of smoothing out the spur energy spurs into a more continuous noise. If the quantization noise is viewed as uniformly distributed white noise, (13.8) simplifies to [2]:

$$|Y_{Noise}(f)| = (2\pi)^2 \cdot \left(2 \cdot \sin\left(\pi \cdot \frac{f}{f_s}\right)\right)^{2 \cdot (n-1)} \cdot \left(\frac{1 \cdot Hz}{12 \cdot f_s}\right) \qquad (13.8)$$

Figure 13-5 shows the theoretical noise spectrum noise spectrum for a delta sigma divider used in a fractional Phased-Locked Loop (PLL) for a sampling frequency of 10 MHz.

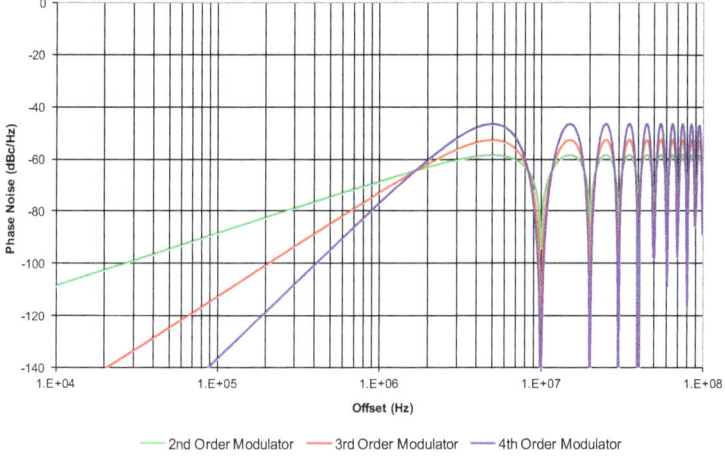

Figure 13-5   *Theoretical Noise of a PLL Delta-Sigma Fractional Divider*

Conclusion

Sampling, analog to digital conversion, and digital to analog conversion are key concepts and used widely in the area of electronics. In the analog world, there are many analog signals such as electromagnetic waves, light, and sound that are sampled and converted from analog to digital. Processing can be done with analog filters, mixers, and other components, but often times it is more effectively done in the digital domain.

By using analog to digital converters, signals can be converted to a stream of numbers that allow many digital processing techniques to be applied. Once all the processing is done in the digital domain, the digital information can be converted back to analog information with the digital to analog converter and used for whatever it is needed for.

References

[1]   http://amo.net/NT/02-21-01FPS.html *gives insight into the sampling rate of the human eye. Retrieved October 28, 2013*

[2]   *Banerjee, Dean "Fractional N Frequency Synthesis" Texas Instruments Application Note AN-1879.   2008*

[3]   *Man, Ching   "Quantization Noise: An Expanded Derivation of the Equation, SNR=6.02n+1.76dB".   Analog Devices Mini Tutorial MT-229. August 2012.*

[4]   *"Demystifying Delta-Sigma ADCs". Maxim Integrated Tutorial 1870. Jan 31, 2003*

[5]   *Gardner, Floyd "Charge Pump Phased Locked Loops". IEEE Transactions on Communications, Vol. COM-28, NO. 11, November 1980*

Chapter 14

Digital Filters

Introduction

Filters are a key component in electronics because they allow the desired frequencies to pass through while blocking out the undesired frequencies. There are many advantages to doing filters in the digital domain such as resistance to process and temperature variations, compact size, and the ability to adjust them in software. This chapter discusses some basics of digital filter design.

Examples of Simple Digital Filters

Perhaps the simplest example of digital filters outside of electronics is the moving average that is used for analyzing stock prices. The moving average is the average of the last *n* values and has the impact of smoothing out the curve so the trends are more easily visible as shown in Figure 14-1.

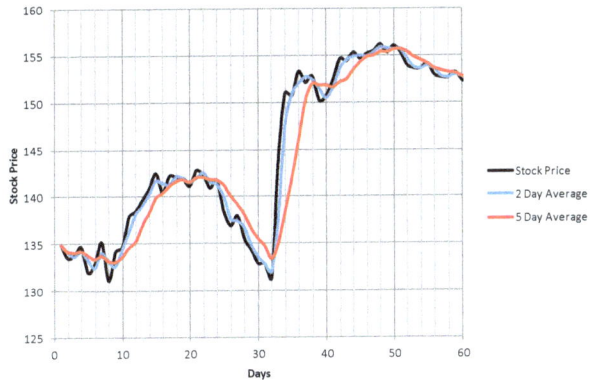

Figure 14-1   *Stock Price Moving Average Example*

The formal equation for the moving average is shown in (14.1).

$$y_n = \frac{\sum_{i=0}^{k-1} x_{n-i}}{k} \tag{14.1}$$

The first step in calculating the frequency response of (14.1) is to take the Z transform.

$$H(z) = \frac{\sum_{i=0}^{k-1} z^{-i}}{k} \quad (14.2)$$

Figure 14-2 shows the frequency response of the transfer function (14.2). As more averages are used, the attenuation at higher frequencies is increased at the expense of a slower response time as shown in Figure 14-1.

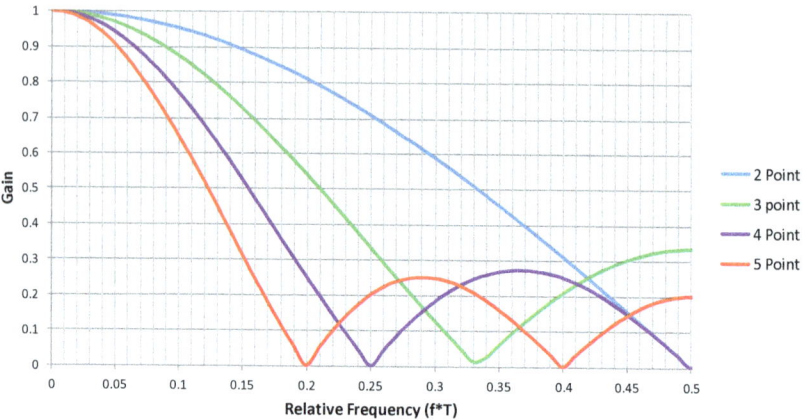

Figure 14-2   *Frequency Response of the Moving Average*

The moving average is perhaps the simplest kind of digital filter, but there are many other varieties of digital filters. For instance, instead of using a moving average, the *recursive filter* takes the weighted average of the last output and the current input as shown in (14.3).

$$y_{n+1} = \alpha \cdot y_n + (1-\alpha) \cdot x_n \quad (14.3)$$

In general, digital filters can be made much more sophisticated than this and the general concept is to consider all filters that can be expressed as the ratio of two polynomials as in (14.4). In this form, the digital filter can be implemented with a series of scaling, summing, and time shifting operations.

$$\frac{Output}{Input} = T(z) = \frac{b_0 + b_1 \cdot z^{-1} + \ldots + b_m \cdot z^{-m}}{a_0 + a_1 \cdot z^{-1} + \ldots + a_k \cdot z^{-k}} \quad (14.4)$$

If the input is x_n and the output is y_n, then equation (14.4) can be expressed as a difference equation.

$$a_0 \cdot y_n + a_1 \cdot y_{n-1} + \ldots + a_n \cdot y_{n-k} = b_0 \cdot x_n + b_1 \cdot x_{n-1} + \ldots + x_n \cdot y_{n-m} \quad (14.5)$$

Transforming Analog Filters to Digital Filters

The Bilinear Transform

One common and intuitive approach to digital filter design is to start with known filter in the analog domain and transform it to an equivalent filter in the digital domain. Although the Z and s domains are exactly related by an elegant closed form equation (12.16), this typically does not lead to an expression that can be expressed as the ratio of two polynomials. The Bilinear transform is an expression that has excellent approximation quality while still allowing the Z domain expression to be expressed as the ratio of two polynomials. The derivation of the Bilinear transform starts out by using the Taylor series for e^x.

$$e^x = 1 + x + \frac{x^2}{2!} + \frac{x^3}{3!} + \ldots \approx 1 + x \tag{14.6}$$

Combining this approximation with the relation between z and s yields a simpler relationship.

$$z = e^{sT} = \frac{e^{sT/2}}{e^{-sT/2}} \approx \frac{1 + s \cdot T/2}{1 - s \cdot T/2} \tag{14.7}$$

Equation (14.7) can be solved for s to create the Bilinear Transform.

$$\frac{2}{T} \cdot \frac{z-1}{z+1} \to s \tag{14.8}$$

Frequency Warping

The Bilinear Transform gives a convenient way to convert between the s and Z domains and keep transfer functions as a ratio of polynomials. Because the Bilinear transform is an approximation, the analog filter frequency, $\hat{\omega}$, is "warped" to a slightly different digital filter frequency, ω. The analog domain frequency can be found by relating the true value of the variable s to the approximated value of it as was found in (14.8).

$$s = j \cdot \hat{\omega} = \frac{2}{T} \cdot \frac{z-1}{z+1} = \frac{2}{T} \cdot \frac{e^{j\omega T} - 1}{e^{j\omega T} + 1} \tag{14.9}$$

This can be written in terms of the tangent function.

$$s = \frac{2}{T} \cdot j \cdot \frac{\left(e^{\frac{j\omega T}{2}} - e^{\frac{-j\omega T}{2}}\right)/(2 \cdot j)}{\left(e^{\frac{j\omega T}{2}} + e^{\frac{-j\omega T}{2}}\right)/2} \qquad (14.10)$$

$$= \frac{2}{T} \cdot j \cdot \tan\left(\omega \cdot \frac{T}{2}\right)$$

Simplifying (14.10) yields an equation that allows one to convert from the analog filter response to the digital filter response.

$$\omega = \frac{2}{T} \cdot \tan^{-1}\left(\hat{\omega} \cdot \frac{T}{2}\right) \qquad (14.11)$$

Figure 14-3 shows the graph of (14.11) with frequencies normalized to the sampling frequency. Although the digital filter frequency is slightly less than the analog filter frequency, it is actually very close. To satisfy the Nyquist criterion, the frequency should be no more than 0.5 times the Nyquist frequency, and at this point, the error due to frequency warping is only about 2%. In other words, the Bilinear Transform is a very good approximation for frequencies of interest.

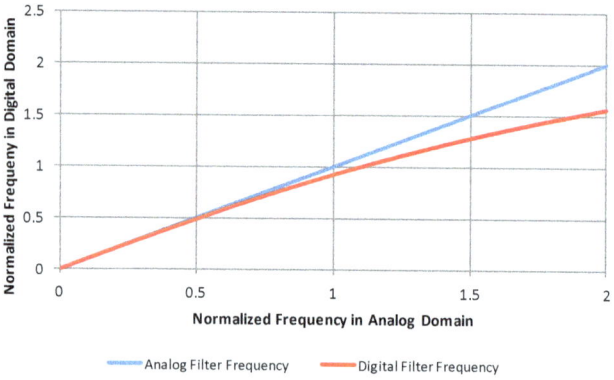

Figure 14-3   Frequency Warping

Often times, the impact of frequency warping is small enough that it is not a major consideration for many applications. However, for those circumstances where the 2% error is not acceptable, one can take frequency warping into account by adjusting the key analog frequency parameter using equation (14.2).

$$\hat{\omega} = \frac{2}{T} \cdot \tan\left(\omega \cdot \frac{T}{2}\right) \qquad (14.12)$$

For example, if the sampling frequency rate was 1 MHz and one wanted to make a digital band pass filter with a bandwidth of 300 kHz, then one would actually design the analog filter to be transformed with a bandwidth of 302.27 kHz so that the digital filter would have the intended bandwidth of 300 kHz.

Tips for Digital Filter Designs Using the Bilinear Transform

There are few things that one should be aware of when using the bilinear transform.

- Be generous using op-amps for the theoretical analog filter design. For analog filters, there may be some aversion to using op-amps for reasons such as cost or noise, but in the digital domain, these are not issues.
- Watch out for instability
  In the analog domain, devices have non-zero output impedances and there are parasitic resistances. Figure 14-4 is a good example of a filter that would work fine in the analog domain, but would be unstable when converted to the digital domain.

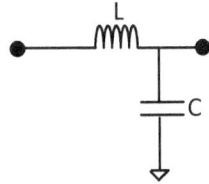

Figure 14-4   *Analog Filter Leading to Instability*

To fix this, it is necessary to put a small parasitic resistance in series with the inductor before converting this to the digital domain.
- For some filter designs, especially band pass and notch filters, it may be necessary to take frequency warping into account by using equation (14.12).
- It is easiest to express center frequencies and bandwidths of filters in terms of the sampling frequency, f_s in order to simplify a lot of the math.

Example – Low Pass RC Filter

One of the simplest low pass filter designs is the low pass RC filter shown in Table 14-4, which has a filter response as follows:

$$H(s) = \frac{1}{1+s \cdot \tau} \qquad (14.13)$$

The bandwidth of this simple low pass filter is related to the parameter τ and is expressed in radians/second. At the bandwidth frequency, the magnitude of the transfer function (14.13) is $1/\sqrt{2}$, which is approximately 0.707. This bandwidth frequency is shown below:

$$\hat{\omega}_c = \frac{1}{\tau} \tag{14.14}$$

Applying the Bilinear transform gives the Z domain equivalent.

$$H(z) = \frac{1}{1+\tau \cdot \frac{2}{T} \cdot \frac{z-1}{z+1}} = \frac{z+1}{\left(1+\frac{2 \cdot \tau}{T}\right) \cdot z + \left(1-\frac{2 \cdot \tau}{T}\right)}$$

$$= \frac{1+z^{-1}}{(1+\alpha)+(1-\alpha) \cdot z^{-1}} \tag{14.15}$$

It is beneficial to introduce the intermediate parameter, α. For this parameter, be aware that f_s is in Hz and $\hat{\omega}_c$ is in radians, so there will be an extra factor of 2π in the denominator.

$$\alpha = \frac{2 \cdot \tau}{T} = 2 \cdot \frac{f_s}{\hat{\omega}_c} \tag{14.16}$$

This yields the final transfer function.

$$H(z) = \frac{1+z^{-1}}{(1+\alpha)+(1-\alpha) \cdot z^{-1}} \tag{14.17}$$

Table 14-3 shows three design examples.

Filter	A	B	C	D
Bandwidth/f_s	0.01	0.1	0.2	0.4
ω_c	0.062832	0.628319	1.256637	2.513274
$\hat{\omega}_c$	0.062853	0.649839	1.453085	6.155367
τ	15.91026	1.538842	0.688191	0.16246
α	31.82052	3.077684	1.376382	0.32492

Table 14-3   Low Pass Filter Example

The frequency response of these three design examples is shown in (14.5). The line near 0.7 gain represents the power bandwidth of these filters.

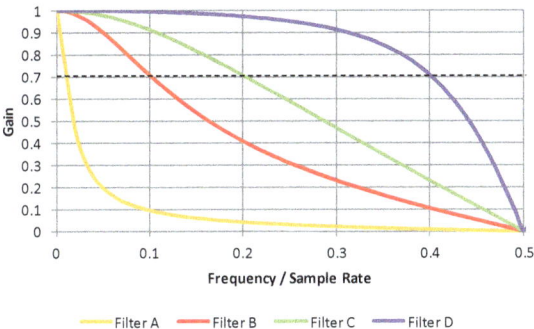

Figure 14-5   *Frequency Responses for Low Pass Filter Example*

The time domain response of the digital filter is obtained by converting (14.18) to a difference equation and solving for the highest order term.

$$\frac{Y(z)}{X(z)} = \frac{1+z^{-1}}{(1+\alpha)+(1-\alpha)\cdot z^{-1}} \tag{14.18}$$

$$y_n = \frac{x_n + x_{n-1} - (1-\alpha)\cdot y_{n-1}}{1+\alpha} \tag{14.19}$$

There is a trade-off between response time and filter attenuation. Comparing the filter response of Filter A to Filter C in Figure 14-6, we see that Filter A attenuates the input signal more at the expense of a slower response time. One advantage of digital filters is that the coefficients for coefficients can be adjusted in software instead of hardware, making the design much more flexible to allow for this kind of trade-off.

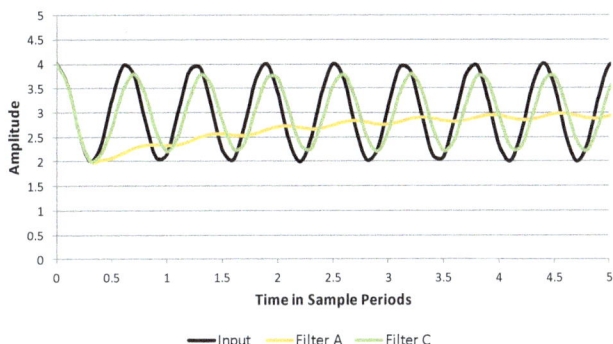

Figure 14-6   *Time Domain Response of Low Pass Filter Example*

Common Filter Types

	Analog Diagram	Analog Filter	Digital Equivalent
Low Pass	R—C (series R to shunt C)	$\dfrac{1}{1+s\cdot\tau}$ $\tau = R\cdot C$	$\dfrac{1+z^{-1}}{(1+\alpha)+(1-\alpha)\cdot z^{-1}}$ $\alpha = \dfrac{2\cdot\tau}{T}$
High Pass	C—R (series C to shunt R)	$\dfrac{s\cdot\tau}{1+s\cdot\tau}$ $\tau = R\cdot C$	$\alpha\cdot\dfrac{1-z^{-1}}{(1+\alpha)+(1-\alpha)\cdot z^{-1}}$ $\alpha = \dfrac{2\cdot\tau}{T}$
Band Pass	C—L—R	$\dfrac{s\cdot R\cdot C}{s^2\cdot L\cdot C + s\cdot R\cdot C + 1}$	$\dfrac{R\cdot C\cdot(1-z^{-2})}{\alpha + \beta\cdot z^{-1} + \gamma\cdot z^{-2}}$ $\alpha = T/2 + \dfrac{2\cdot L\cdot C}{T} + R\cdot C$ $\beta = T - \dfrac{4\cdot L\cdot C}{T}$ $\gamma = T/2 + \dfrac{2\cdot L\cdot C}{T} - R\cdot C$
Notch	R—C—L	$\dfrac{1+s^2\cdot L\cdot C}{s^2\cdot L\cdot C + s\cdot C\cdot R + 1}$	$\dfrac{\alpha + \beta\cdot z^{-1} + \alpha\cdot z^{-2}}{(\alpha+\gamma)+\beta\cdot z^{-1}+(\alpha-\gamma)\cdot z^{-2}}$ $\alpha = T^2 + 4\cdot L\cdot C$ $\beta = 2\cdot T^2 - 8\cdot L\cdot C$ $\gamma = 2\cdot R\cdot C\cdot T$

Table 14-4   Analog and Digital Filter Equivalents

Table 14-4 shows some simple filters in the analog domain and their digital equivalents. They can be derived in a very similar way that the low pass filter response was derived.

Example – Butterworth Filter

The *Butterworth filter* is a low pass filter one that contains op-amps and is more complicated than the passive filters discussed so far, but it has better characteristics, especially as more stages are added. As the stages approach infinity, this filter approaches an ideal brick wall filter. The Butterworth filter has the transfer characteristic of:

$$\frac{1}{B_n\left(\dfrac{s}{\omega_c}\right)} \qquad (14.20)$$

B_n is the Butterworth polynomial with coefficients is given by Table 14-5, which was taken from reference [3] that includes polynomials up to 10th order.

Order	Butterworth Polynomial, $B_n(x)$
1	$x+1$
2	$x^2 + 1.4142 \cdot x + 1$
3	$x^3 + 2 \cdot x^2 + 2 \cdot x + 1$
4	$(x^2 + 0.7654 \cdot x + 1) \cdot (x^2 + 1.8478 \cdot x + 1)$
5	$(x+1) \cdot (x^2 + 0.6180 \cdot x + 1) \cdot (x^2 + 1.6180 \cdot x + 1)$
6	$(x^2 + 0.5176 \cdot x + 1) \cdot (x^2 + 1.4142 \cdot x + 1) \cdot (x^2 + 1.9319 \cdot x + 1)$

Table 14-5 *Butterworth Polynomials*

Suppose we wanted a third order digital Butterworth filter with bandwidth of $\hat{\omega}_c$. The first step is use Table 14-5 to create the transfer function in the analog domain.

$$H(s) = \frac{1}{1 + 2 \cdot \left(\frac{s}{\omega_c}\right) + 2 \cdot \left(\frac{s}{\omega_c}\right)^2 + \left(\frac{s}{\omega_c}\right)^3} \tag{14.21}$$

Applying the bilinear transform to (14.21) yields the transfer function in the digital domain.

$$H(z) = \frac{1}{1 + 2 \cdot \left(\frac{2}{T \cdot \omega_c} \cdot \frac{z-1}{z+1}\right) + 2 \cdot \left(\frac{2}{T \cdot \omega_c} \cdot \frac{z-1}{z+1}\right)^2 + \left(\frac{2}{T \cdot \omega_c} \cdot \frac{z-1}{z+1}\right)^3} \tag{14.22}$$

$$H(z) = \frac{1 + 3 \cdot z^{-1} + 3 \cdot z^{-2} + z^{-3}}{A + B \cdot z^{-1} + C \cdot z^{-2} + D \cdot z^{-3}} \tag{14.23}$$

$$\alpha = 2 \cdot \frac{f_s}{\omega_c} \tag{14.24}$$

$$A = 1 + 2 \cdot \alpha + 2 \cdot \alpha^2 + \alpha^3 \tag{14.25}$$

$$B = 3 + 2 \cdot \alpha - 2 \cdot \alpha^2 - 3 \cdot \alpha^3 \tag{14.26}$$

$$C = 3 - 2 \cdot \alpha - 2 \cdot \alpha^2 + 3 \cdot \alpha^3 \tag{14.27}$$

$$D = 1 - 2 \cdot \alpha + 2 \cdot \alpha^2 - \alpha^3 \tag{14.28}$$

For practical demonstration of how to apply these equations, consider a digital filter design for a 90 kHz cut-off frequency and a sampling rate of 1 MHz.

Parameter	Value
Sampling Rate, f_s	1 MHz
Bandwidth, BW	90 kHz
BW / f_s	0.09
ω_c	0.56549 Mrad / s
$\hat{\omega}_c$	0.58105 Mrad / s
α	3.4420
A	72.3585
B	−136.1493
C	94.7592
D	−22.9684

Table 14-6   Butterworth Filter Calculation

The final transfer function is shown below and the frequency response is in Figure 14-7.

$$\frac{1 + 3 \cdot z^{-1} + 3 \cdot z^{-2} + z^{-3}}{72.3585 - 136.1493 \cdot z^{-1} + 94.7592 \cdot z^{-2} - 22.9684 \cdot z^{-3}} \quad (14.29)$$

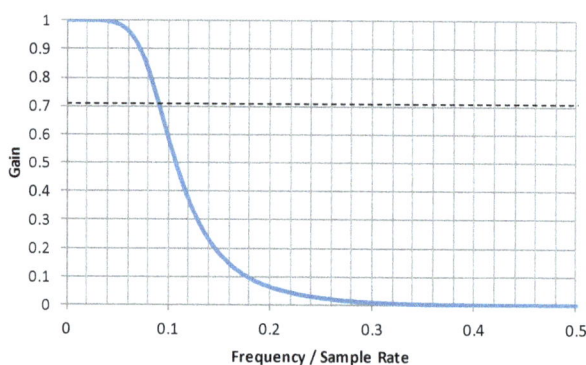

Figure 14-7   Butterworth Filter Response

A Butterworth Digital Filter to Analyze Stocks Instead of a Moving Average?

A comparison between Figure 14-7 and Figure 14-2 shows that the Butterworth filter has a similar bandwidth, but a much sharper roll-off. Indeed the moving average can be made to smooth out the stock price more, but Figure 14-1 demonstrates that then the response time will be slower. This begs the question as to whether a Butterworth filter might be able to smooth out the curve better with less delay. It turns out that if the bandwidth is the same, the digital Butterworth filter seems to add more delay. However, if the bandwidth is increased to compensate for this, then the response time can be improved and steeper roll-off will still be effective at filtering. Figure 14-8 implies that perhaps this is true and shows the Butterworth filter with the bandwidth of 0.25 samples/day has a faster response than the 5 day moving average and still gives a nice smooth curve that can be used for analysis.

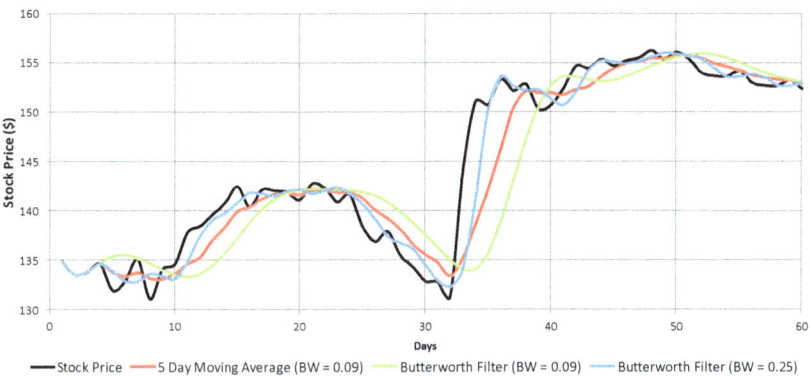

Figure 14-8   *Butterworth Filter vs. Moving Average for Stock Price Analysis*

Digital Filter Implementation

Implementation is not much of an issue for digital filters that are created on a computer or means where the software is very flexible However, if it is done with electronic components, then diagrams are typically used to show the series of add, multiply, and time shift operations as shown in Figure 14-9.

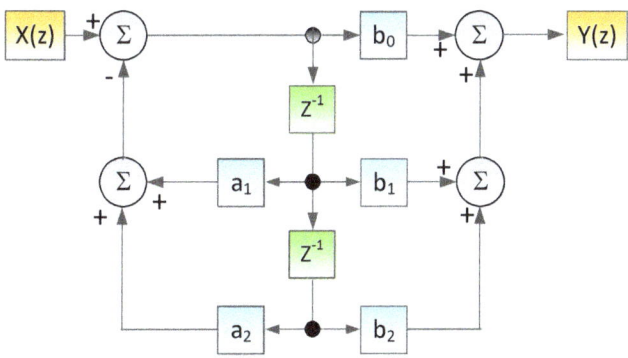

Figure 14-9   *Diagram of a Digital Filter*

Conclusion

In summary, although there is an exact closed form relationship between z and s, the Bilinear transform is still a useful approximation because it leads to transfer functions that can expressed as the ratio of two polynomials which is easier to implement. The following table shows some of the various approximations that can be used along with their effectiveness.

Quality	Approximation	Comments
Worst	$z \rightarrow 1$ as $s \rightarrow 0$	Good only to find DC response
Poor	$z \rightarrow 1+s$	Typically not used, but shows up when relating Z and s transforms.
Excellent (Bilinear Transform)	$z = \dfrac{1+s \cdot T/2}{1-s \cdot T/2}$	Equivalent to a 3 term Taylor series and is very good and leads to transfer functions that are the ratio of two polynomials
Exact	$z = e^{s \cdot T}$	This is the exact relationship and used for calculating the frequency response.

Table 14-7   Approximations Used for Digital Filters

Many of the concepts for analog filter design can be extended to digital filters. There are techniques that can only be done in the digital domain, but this is beyond the scope of this book.

References

[1]   "Bilinear Transform" Wikipedia. Retrieved October 28, 2013 from http://en.wikipedia.org/wiki/Bilinear_transform

[2]   "Digital Filters" Nuhertz. Retrieved October 28, 2013 from http://bfilter-solutions.com/digital.html

[3]   "Butterworth Filter, Tutorial 8 of 8" Retrieved October 28, 2013 from http://www.electronics-tutorials.ws/filter/filter_8.html

Chapter 15

Digital Communications

Introduction

Converting information from analog to digital formats allows the information to be better stored and transmitted over wires or through the air. The earliest digital communications, such as the *telegraph*, were likely designed the way they were in order to simplify the transmitter and the receiver. For more modern communications, the motivations for doing so are not so much simplicity, but improved signal quality, improved resistance to noise, improved spectral efficiency, and the ability to add encryption.

The First Digital Communications – the Telegraph

The telegraph is perhaps the first instance of widely adopted digital communications. The general principle is the two communicating parties are at opposite ends of a long wire and a voltage is switched on and off in order that it can be detected on the opposite end with either a light bulb flashing, a voltmeter, or a device that can make a series of clicks whenever this voltage is applied. Typically there is a key or button that is pressed to make these clicks.

Perhaps the earliest and most simple communication language for the telegraph was *Morse code*. Morse code is a series information represented by dots and dashes. The dot is a quick pulse and the dash is longer pulse, typically on the order of three times the length of the dot. Messages could be formed by these dots and dashes.

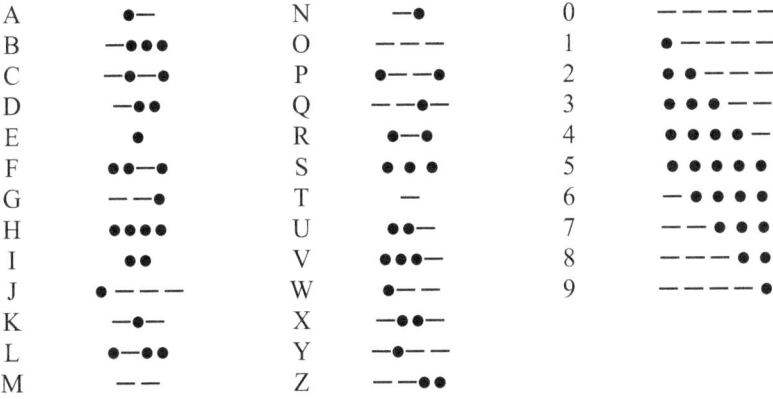

Figure 15-1 Morse Code

Morse code has the advantages that it is very easy to implement and usable in many situations where other forms of communications may not be possible. Aside from sending these messages over a wire, it can be done by turning lights on and off, tapping on a scuba tank underwater, blinking one's eyes, and a vast host of other situations.

Communications Using a Modulated Carrier

Using a Carrier for Communications

The telegraph was a simple way of sending a message from one person to another over a wire. However, the situation might not be so simple if there were multiple people trying to use the same wire. Even better than multiple users using the same wire would be the ability to transmit messages through the air. If a sinusoidal voltage is produced with high enough power and used with a transmitting antenna, this signal, called a *carrier*, can be sent through the air and picked up by a receiving antenna. If amplitude, phase, or frequency of the carrier is *modulated*, then information can be sent over the air without the aid of connecting wires. By using multiple carriers it is possible to have simultaneous communications between multiple parties. Because of this fact, carriers are often also used a broad variety of wired communications, such as cable TV.

Amplitude Modulation

Amplitude modulation (AM) refers to modulating the carrier with amplitude information. In general, a carrier using amplitude modulation is of the form:

$$v(t) = A(t) \cdot \sin(2\pi \cdot f_{carrier} \cdot t) \tag{15.1}$$

Analog AM modulation is relatively simple and used in many applications, such as AM radio. In this case, *A(t)* is a waveform representing the sound being transmitted.

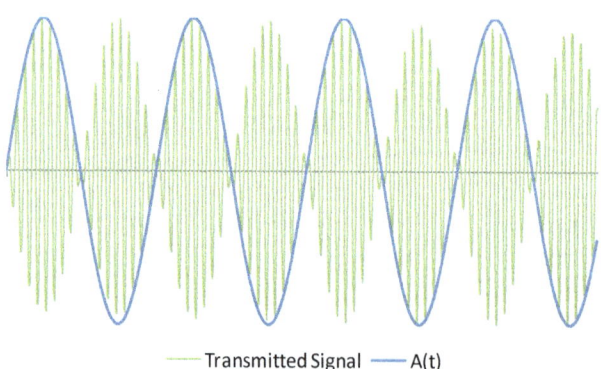

Figure 15-2   *Analog Amplitude Modulation*

Digital amplitude modulation is done by changing the amplitude *A(t)* between a set of discrete values. The simplest form of digital analog modulation is known as *on-off keying,* where the two states are on and off. The wireless telegraph is a good example of something that used on-off keying. A more modern example of this might be the garage door opener, which uses on-off digital AM modulation to produce a code that can be interpreted. This code needs to be sophisticated enough that it is not easy to be guessed by criminals and there is not interference between different garage door openers.

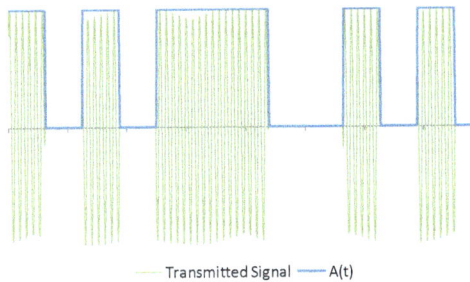

Figure 15-3   *On-Off Keying Example*

Frequency Modulation

Frequency modulation (FM) works by changing the carrier frequency by a small amount in order to transmit information. Although it is typically a little more complicated than AM modulation, it is often preferred because it has a much higher immunity to noise. FM modulation has the following form.

$$v(t) = sin(2\pi \cdot [f_{carrier} + F(t)] \cdot t) \tag{15.2}$$

One of the more familiar applications of analog FM modulation is FM radio. In this case, *A(t)* is a waveform representing the sound that is being transmitted.

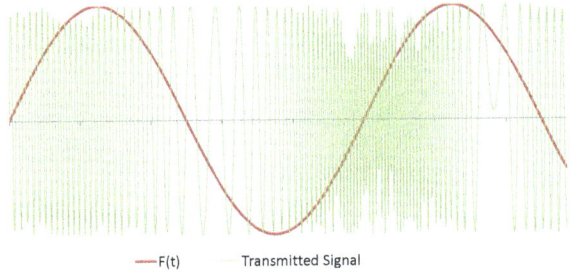

Figure 15-4   *FM Modulation*

Digital FM modulation is done by making *A(t)* change between a series of discrete states and is often referred to as *Frequency Shift Keying (FSK)*.

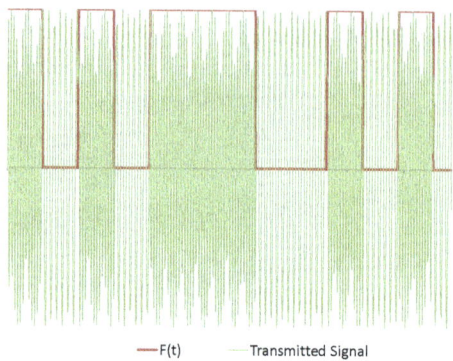

Figure 15-5   *FSK Example*

It can be shown that phase is the integral of frequency, so it is common for textbooks to consider FM modulation as a special class of *phase modulation*.

IQ Modulation

IQ modulation is a general class of modulation in which both the amplitude and the phase are changed. There is no analog equivalent of this. The advantage of IQ modulation is that it allows more information to be modulated on the carrier in order to minimize the bandwidth of spectrum that is needed.

$$v(t) = I(t) \cdot \sin(f_{carrier} \cdot t) + Q(t) \cdot \cos(f_{carrier} \cdot t) \tag{15.3}$$

I(t) and *Q(t)* can be varied between a set of discrete states. For instance, *Quadrature Phase Shift Keying (QPSK)* allows *I* and *Q* to be varied between the states of 0 and 1. So at each instance in time, a symbol can be sent that has 4 states, which allows twice the information to be sent in the same bandwidth.

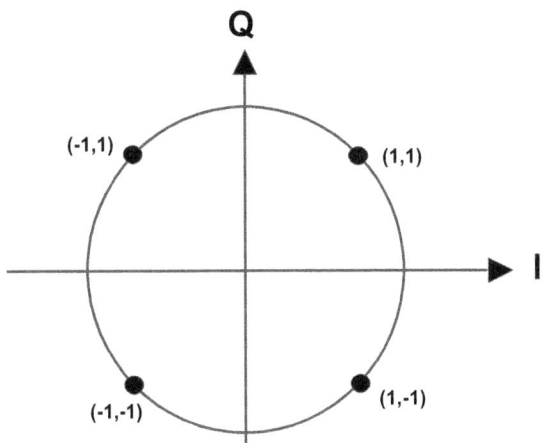

Table 15-3 *QPSK Constellation*

Another example of IQ modulation is *Quadrature Amplitude Modulation (QAM)*. There are many varieties of QAM. For instance, 256 QAM has 16 states for ***I*** and 16 states for ***Q***. Having 256 states per symbol means that the amount of information that can be sent in the same bandwidth is theoretically increased by a factor of $\log_2(256) = 8$.

Multiple Access Techniques

Multiple access refers to multiple users using the same medium for communications at the same time, whether it is a wire or the air.

Time Division

To allow for multiple users to use the same medium simultaneously, dividing up the message in time slots can be used. For example, in the telegraph, the same wire could be used for both transmitting and sending a signal provided that both users were not trying to transmit at the same time. Another simple example of this might be walkie-talkies that have a "talk" button by dividing up timeframe into multiple slots and alternating the slots for talk and receive. This is sometimes referred to as *Time Division Duplexing*. When there is more than just two time slots for talk and receive, *TDMA (Time Division Multiple Access)* can be used as shown in Figure 15-6. For this, there is typically some timeframe that is divided up into segments for each user to use.

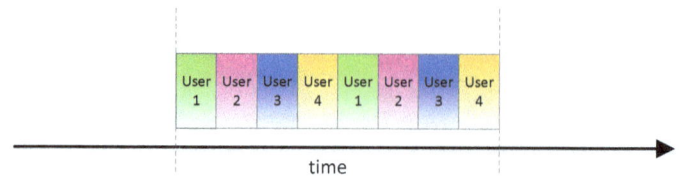

Figure 15-6   *Time Division Multiple Access*

Frequency Division

Another method to allow for multiple users to use the same medium simultaneously is to use multiple frequencies. The simplest example might be if a user has one frequency to transmit a message and then receives the response on a different frequency. Typically, there is a total bandwidth of spectrum available for the whole system and different frequency bands are given to each user as shown in Figure 15-7.

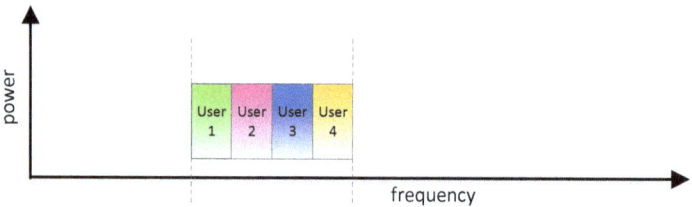

Figure 15-7   *Frequency Division Multiple Access*

If the message is digitally encoded, then it is possible to hop between multiple frequencies with a technique known as *frequency hopping*. The advantage of frequency hopping is that it makes the messages much less vulnerable to interference and also ensures that the allocated spectrum is used more efficiently. This is sometimes referred to as *frequency hopping spread spectrum* because this spreads out the information over the whole bandwidth of the system.

Code Division Multiple Access

CDMA *(Code Division Multiple Access)* is a standard that uses several orthogonal codes. This method can only be used with digital communications and has the advantage that it has higher noise immunity, uses the entire available spectrum more efficiently, and also is better for secure communications.

The basic concept is to combine the intended message with *orthogonal functions*, such as the *Walsh functions*. The useful property of these functions is that when two of them are multiplied together, the result is zero if the functions were different and nonzero if they were the same.

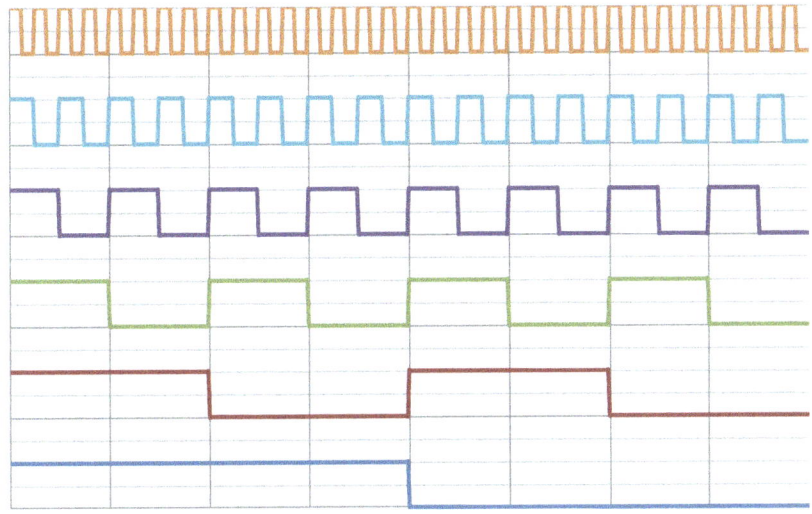

Figure 15-8   *Six Different Walsh Functions*

The concept for CDMA communications is the multiply each separate intended message by an orthogonal function, such as the Walsh function. The total message is the sum of all the messages. At the receiving end, the received total message is multiplied by the corresponding orthogonal function to get the original message.

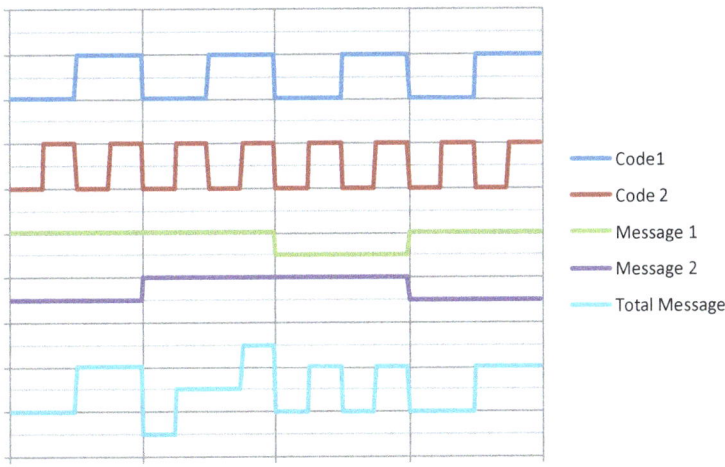

Figure 15-9   *Example of CDMA Coded Message*

To a user who is unaware of the codes, this communication just looks like random noise, but the reality is that this noise is not random and the true signal can be extracted from it. CDMA communications have the advantages that there is higher security, more resistance to jamming, and also it makes more efficient use of the spectrum by completely using all that is available and wasting none. Because the encoding spreads the signal out over the available bandwidth, CDMA is sometimes referred to as *direct sequence spread spectrum*. CDMA standards today actually use sophisticated codes than shown in this example, but the general concept is similar.

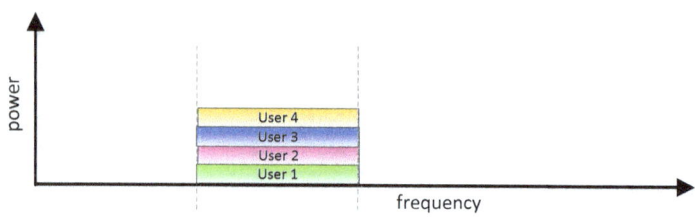

Figure 15-10   *CDMA Example*

For actual CDMA communications, such as those used in cellular phones, the actual encoding scheme is far more sophisticated than what was presented here, but the general concept still applies.

Error Correction

One advantage of digital communications is that it allows *error correction*. Perhaps the simplest method is the *parity check*. The basic concept of this is that the message is comprised of 1's and 0's. At the end of the message, the parity check bit is added to indicate if this sum is even or odd. If there is a single error in transmission, then the parity check bit will be off and the message can be retransmitted.

Although the parity check may work and is used in many applications, it may not be desirable to retransmit the message again. Also, the parity check can be fooled if there is an even number of errors.

The concept of *forward error correction* is to send redundant information that can be used to correct the message if there are errors. The simplest example of this may be to send each bit multiple times. For example, if the message was 1 0 1 1 0 0 1, then one might send 1 1 1 0 0 0 1 1 1 1 1 1 0 0 0 0 0 0 1 1 1. If there is a discrepancy between the three bits, one can just take the two bits that agree that correct the error. Because the *bit error rate* tends to be much smaller than one, this error correction greatly reduces the probability of error. Table 15-4 compares this error correction strategy of using three bits to using no error correction. To a first order approximation if the probably of error with no correction is *p* then the error correction reduces this probability from *p* to $3 \cdot p^2$, which is a substantial reduction.

Number of Errors	No Error Correction	3 Bit Redundancy
0	$1-p$	$(1-p)^3$
1	p	$3 \cdot p \cdot (1-p)^2$
2	—	$3 \cdot p^2 \cdot (1-p)$
3	—	p^3
Total Probability	p	$3 \cdot p^2 - 2 \cdot p^3 \approx 3 \cdot p^2$

Table 15-4   *Error Correction Example*

Figure 15-11 shows this error correction applied to this example with sending three bits instead of one.

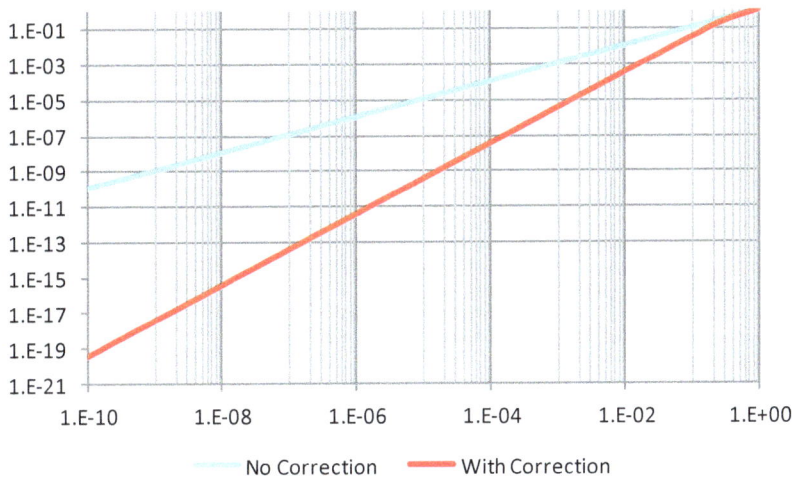

Figure 15-11   *Impact of Error Correction*

Error correction is very effective in reducing the number of errors, but it comes at the cost of reducing the transmission speed. In the previous example, the transmission rate would be one third, since three bits were sent instead of one. For applications where transmission rate is really not much of a concern, such as a garage door opener, this is acceptable. However, if it was an application such as voice over a cellular phone or data over the internet, this slower transmission speed might be more of a concern. This technique of using three bits instead of one is not very efficient and there are more efficient methods, such as *Hamming Codes*.

In general, errors in transmission or digital storage have a tendency to come in clusters, as would be the case for something like errors caused by a scratch on a CD. This makes it much more likely to get two or more errors in a row and cause a transmission error. In order to mitigate this, *interleaving* can be used. The general concept of interleaving is to scramble the information stream in a known way so that a cluster of errors can be handled by the error correction. For instance, if the message was "hello", one might send the message "hhheeellllllooo". In this case, a single error could be corrected. However, if there were two errors in a row, there would be a problem. If instead the message "hellohellohello" was sent, then a sequence of errors of length five or less could still be tolerated.

Conclusion

Digital communications has many advantages over analog communications and is the direction that things are going. The examples in this chapter were very basic to illustrate the key concepts. There are much more sophisticated methods that can be far more involved and are beyond the scope of this book.

Appendix

Table of Symbols

Symbol	Meaning
$\equiv$	Denotes that two numbers are equivalent modulo some number.
π	The mathematical constant approximately equal to 3.1415926…
$\sharp$	Musical Sharp
$\prod_{i=1}^{n} x_i$	Finite product of $x_1 \cdot x_2 \cdot \ldots \cdot x_n$
$\flat$	Musial Flat
$\begin{vmatrix} a & b \\ c & d \end{vmatrix}$	Vertical bars are used to denote the determinant of a matrix. For this example on the left, it would be $a \cdot d - b \cdot c$.
$\bullet$	Dot product. Used for matrix or vector multiplication.
$\cdot$ or $\times$	Multiplication
ω	Frequency expressed in radians
ω_c	Bandwidth expressed in radians
e	The mathematical constant approximately equal to 2.7182818…
f	Frequency expressed in Hz
f_s	Sampling Frequency
f_c	Bandwidth expressed in Hz
GCD	Greatest Common Divisor
i or j	The mathematical constant equal to $\sqrt{-1}$
LCM	Least Common multiple
mod	Modulo operator
$\sum_{i=1}^{n} x_i$	Summation equal to $x_1 + x_2 + \ldots x_n$
T	Sample Period
$\vec{x}$	The vector x.
$\hat{x}$	A different version of x, perhaps x multiplied by some constant.

Glossary

aliasing
The process of creating an erroneous "alias" frequency from a sampled signal at an insufficient rate.

analog to digital converter (ADC)
An electronic component that converts a time-varying analog voltage into a stream of numbers.

analog to digital converter, delta sigma
An analog to digital converter that uses a high sample rate with low resolution in its initial stage to improve performance. The sample rate is then decreased and resolution improved with the decimation filter.

bandwidth
This can either mean a continuous range of frequencies or a filter bandwidth. The filter bandwidth is the range of frequencies that can pass through without being attenuated too much. In this book, it is assumed that the magnitude of the transfer function is $1/\sqrt{2}$ at the bandwidth frequency, although other references might use a different magnitude.

bit
A value for transmitted or stored information that assumes the states of 1 or 0.

bit error
An error in decoding a bit that was transmitted. For instance, if a 0 was sent and it was incorrectly interpreted as a 1, this would be considered a bit error.

bit error rate (BER)
The frequency of occurrence for bit errors.

bang bang control system
A control system that works with only two states.

Bilinear Transform
A mathematical transform used to convert an analog transfer function, such as that from a filter, to the digital domain.

carrier
A high frequency wave used to transmit signals.

chord
A musical term referring to three or more notes played together.

chord, major
A chord of three notes played together such that the second note is a third above the lowest note and the third note is a fifth above the lowest note.

chord, minor
A chord of three notes such that the second note is a minor third above the lowest note and the third note is fifth above the lowest note.

Circle of Fifths
A musical term for a visual representation used to remember key signatures by placing them in a circle.

Coin Problem
A problem asking what is the smallest value that cannot be attained using a combination of coins of fixed denominations.

dead band
In a digital three-state control system, this is an area where the correction is very small and may be undetectable or less than other tolerances of the system

dead zone
An area near zero phase error in a phase detector of where small errors cannot be properly detected.

derivative
A mathematical term for taking the slope of a curve about a point.

determinant
A number calculated from a square matrix. If the determinant is nonzero, the inverse of the matrix exists.

discrete arithmetic
Arithmetic that involves sets that are restricted to discrete values.

duplexing
The action of combining two signals on a single channel in order to allow communication in both directions.

duplexing, frequency division (FDD)
Duplexing that uses different frequencies to combine two signals.

duplexing, time division (TDD)
Duplexing that uses different time slots to combine two signals.

equivalence class
The set of all numbers that are equivalent some modulus, M.

Eigenvalue and Eigenvector
The concept is that for an eigenvector, $\vec{x}$, of a matrix, M, the product of the matrix and the eigenvector is a scalar, λ, times the eigenvector. The scalar is called the eigenvalue. The general relationship is given as follows:
$$A \bullet \vec{x} = \lambda \bullet \vec{x}$$

error correction
The process of correcting communication errors that were transmitted.

error correction, forward (FEC)
A type of error correction that that corrects errors as they come, as opposed to waiting for the entire message to be transmitted and then correcting.

Euclidean Algorithm
A method of finding the greatest common divisor of two numbers by successively looking at the difference of the two numbers.

evenly spaced set
A set where if the elements are arranged from least to greatest, the spacing between each element and the next larger one is the same.

equation, difference
An equation involving unknown functions that are defined only at discrete values.

equation, differential
An equation involving derivatives of unknown functions.

equation, diophantine
An equation where the solution is restricted to integers.

Equation, Frobenius
An linear equation where the solutions are restricted to nonnegative integers.

equation, integer
An equation where the solutions are restricted to integers, also known as a diophantine equation.

equation, modular (modulus)
An equation involving the modulus operator.

equation, Pell's
A diophantine equation of the form $x^2 - a \cdot y^2 = 1$.

Euler's Identity
A key relationship in mathematics that links the complex number, *i*, the mathematical constant, *e*, and the trigonometric functions as follows:
$$e^{i \cdot x} = \cos(x) + i \cdot \sin(x)$$

Fibonacci Sequence
A well known sequence in mathematics in which the next term is formed by adding the two previous terms. The sequence is 1, 1, 2, 3, 5, 8, 13,...

fifth
A musical term referring to seven half steps, which is approximately a factor of 1.5 in frequency.

filter
An electronic component that reduces the power of the input signal in a certain range of frequency.

filter, analog
A filter that works with an analog frequency as the input.

filter, anti-aliasing
A filter that reduces the undesired alias frequency.

filter, band pass
A filter that attenuates all frequencies that are not in a certain band.

filter, Butterworth
A low pass filter optimized for a flat frequency response for frequencies below and near the bandwidth.

filter, decimation
A filter that combines several samples of low resolution into one of higher resolution. For instance, a decimation filter might take four one-bit samples and combine into one four-bit sample.

filter, digital
A filter that works with digital data as the input.

filter, high pass
A filter that attenuates frequencies below its bandwidth.

filter, low pass
A filter that attenuates frequencies above its bandwidth.

filter, notch
A filter that attenuates only frequencies that are in a certain band.

filter, recursive
A digital filter that calculates the output as a weighted average of the current input and previous output.

finite difference
The difference between the next incremental value of a function and the current value, $f_{n+1} - f_n$.

flat (♭)
A musical term meaning to decrease the note frequency by one half step.

Fourier Series
A representation of for periodic functions using sin and cosine basis functions or complex exponential basis functions.

$$f(x) = \frac{a_0}{2} + \sum_{n=1}^{\infty}\left[a_n \cdot \cos\left(\frac{2 \cdot n \cdot \pi \cdot x}{L}\right) + b_n \cdot \sin\left(\frac{2 \cdot n \cdot \pi \cdot x}{L}\right)\right] = \sum_{n=1}^{\infty} c_n \cdot e^{i\left(\frac{2 \cdot n \cdot \pi \cdot x}{L}\right)}$$

fractional frequency divider
A divider that can divide the input frequency by a fractional value.

frequency
A term referring to the number of oscillations per second. For instance, f is the frequency for the sine wave $y = \sin(f \cdot t)$.

frequency warping
A distortion in the frequency caused by the bilinear transform.

Frobenius Number
The smallest number that can not be expressed as a positive linear combination of two or more numbers.

Golden Mean
A number in that comes up in various mathematical situations and is equal to $\frac{1+\sqrt{5}}{2}$.

greatest common divisor (GCD)
The largest number that will divide a set of one or more numbers.

Hamming Codes
A set of digital codes that can be used in forward error correction.

hysteresis
The use of two thresholds instead of one for preventing undesired oscillation.

integers
A set including the whole numbers and their counterparts that are in the set
$...-3,-2,-1,0,1,2,3,...$

integral
A mathematical operation equated to finding the area under the curve.

interleaving
A method of error correction in which redundant bits are scrambled so that it can be more resistant to multiple bit errors in a row.

interval
A musical term meaning the number of half steps.

Jury's Test
A test that can be used for digital systems to determine if they are stable.

key signature
A musical term referring to the scale on which a musical piece was based on or created.

keying
A type of digital modulation in which the amplitude, frequency, or phase of the carrier is shifted by two or more values.

keying, frequency shift (FSK)
A type of digital modulation in which the frequency of the carrier is shifted by two or more values. Typically, FSK refers to the case when only two frequencies are used and k-FSK refers to the case that more than two frequencies are used, such as 4-FSK.

keying, on-off
A basic form of digital modulation in which the carrier is switched on and off.

keying, phase shift (PSK)
Digital modulation where the phase is shifted between two or more states.

keying, quadrature phase shift (QPSK)
A type of phase shift keying with 4 total states. It is a case of IQ modulation where I and Q both have 2 states.

Laplace transform
A transform in mathematics that maps a signal from the frequency domain to the Laplace (s) domain.

$$F(s) = \int_0^\infty f(t) \cdot e^{-st} \cdot dt$$

Least Common Multiple (LCM)
The smallest number that is a common multiple to a set of one or more numbers.

lowest terms fraction
A fraction where the numerator and denominator have no common factors.

Mandelbrot Set
A set of complex numbers in that yield bounded outputs for a particular difference equation that is discussed in more detail elsewhere in this book.

minimum continuous divide ratio
The smallest division ratio a frequency divider can achieve without having discontinuities any values not allowed that are less than the maximum achievable value for the divider.

modular inverse
The modular inverse of the number a modulo M is denoted as a^{-1} and satisfies the relationship that $a \cdot a^{-1} \equiv 1 \ (mod \ M)$.

modular square root
x is said to be the modular square root of a modulo m if $x^2 \equiv a \ (mod \ m)$.

modulus (mod) operator
An operator meaning to take the remainder after two numbers are divided.

modulation
The action of changing the amplitude, frequency, or phase of a signal. In communications, this is typically done to the carrier; for delta sigma modulation, this is typically done to the data before it is applied to the carrier.

modulation, amplitude (AM)
Modulation that changes the amplitude of the carrier.

modulation, delta sigma
A process of modulating value between many values in order to improve the noise spectrum.

modulation, frequency (FM)
Modulation that changes the frequency of the carrier. This is sometimes considered a special case of phase modulation, because frequency is the derivative of phase.

modulation, IQ
Modulation that uses a linear combination of two signals that are 90 degrees out of phase (in quadrature), which are denoted as I and Q.

modulation, phase (PM)
Modulation that changes the phase of the carrier.

modulation, quadrature amplitude (QAM)
A specific type of IQ modulation in which I and Q have at least 2 states. For instance, 256 QAM refers to the case where both I and Q can assume 16 values, thus leading to 256 states.

Morse Code
A system of communications using the two states of dot and dash to form symbols for letters and numbers.

multiple access
A method of sharing the same communication channel between two or more transmitted messages.

multiple access, code division (CDMA)
A method of multiple access using orthogonal codes to separate the multiple messages being sent.

multiple access, frequency division (FDMA)
A method of multiple access using different frequencies to separate the multiple messages being sent. *FDMA* also can refer to a specific communication standard that uses this technique.

multiple access, time division (TDMA)
A method of multiple access using different slots in time to separate the multiple messages being sent. *TDMA* also can refer to a specific communication standard that uses this technique.

nonharmonious
A musical term for two or more notes that are not nicely related in frequency.

Nyquist rate
The minimum frequency necessary to avoid having any alias frequencies. It is equal to twice the highest frequency component of the sampled frequency.

octave
A musical term referring to 12 half steps, which is exactly a factor of two in frequency.

oscillation
The action of continuously changing between two more states.

oversampling
The action of sampling at frequencies above the Nyquist rate.

parity check
A simple form of error detection in which all the bits in the stream are added up to determine if the sum is even or odd.

prescaler
A simple frequency divider that divides higher frequencies to lower ones

prescaler, dual modulus
A frequency divider consisting of two prescalers that work in conjunction.

prime
A whole number of 2 or greater that has no factors other than 1 and itself.

prime, relatively
A set of two or more numbers that have no factors in common, besides one.

primes, twin
A set of two prime numbers that are exactly two apart.

Pythagorean Triple
A set of three whole numbers, (a,b,c), such that all three numbers are greater than two and a² + b² = c².

Pythagorean Triple, Primitive
A Pythagorean triple of relatively prime numbers.

quantization
The process of converting a continuous signal to a stream of discrete values.

Riemann Sum
A sum used to approximate an integral.

root mean square (RMS)
A type of average value calculated as :

$$F(s) = \sqrt{\frac{\int_a^b f^2(t) \cdot dt}{b-a}}$$

sampling
The process of taking measurements of a signal at discrete intervals of time.

scale
A musical term for a sequence of notes played in ascending order.

scale, major
A musical scale based on a major chord with the notes planed in the sequence whole step, whole step, half step, whole step, whole step, whole step, half step.

scale, minor
A musical scale based on a minor chord with the notes planed in the sequence whole step, half step, whole step, whole step, half step, whole step, whole step.

sharp (#)
A musical term meaning to increase the note by one half step.

solution, homogenous
A complete solution for a difference /differential equation with no constant term.

solution, particular
A specific solution for a difference/differential equation that has a constant term.

spectrum
The frequency representation of a signal with the frequency on the x axis and the power on the y axis.

spread spectrum
A method of spreading the information over a wider transmission bandwidth.

spread spectrum, direct sequence
A method of achieving spread spectrum by combining the transmitted signal with a sequence of orthogonal, or near orthogonal codes.

spread spectrum, frequency hopping
Spread spectrum modulation that is achieved by rapidly changing between different frequencies.

spurs
Undesired noise energy concentrated at a discrete frequencies.

step, half
A musical term indicating an increase (or decrease) in frequency by a factor of $2^{1/12}$, which is approximately 1.06.

step, whole
A musical term meaning an increase or decrease in frequency by a factor of $2^{1/6}$, which is approximately 1.22.

telegraph
A device capable of sending electrical signals over long distances Morse code.

third
A musical term for a four half steps, which is about a factor of 5/4 in frequency.

third, minor
A musical term for a three half steps, which is about a factor of 6/5 in frequency.

variable gain amplifier
An electronic component that has a gain that can be adjusted.

whole number
A number in the set 0,1,2,3,...

Z Transform
A transform in mathematics that maps a signal from the discrete time domain to the Z domain. It is calculated as follows:
$$F(z)=\sum_{n=0}^{\infty} f(n) \cdot z^{-n}$$

Index

Aliasing	109, 142
Amplitude modulation	130
Analog to Digital Converter	107, 142
anti-aliasing filter	110
bang bang control	112, 142
Bilinear Transform	119, 120, 121, 128, 142
bit error	136, 142
Butterworth filter	124, 125, 126
carrier	130, 131, 132, 142, 147, 148, 149
Chinese Remainder Theorem	25, 27
chord	34, 35, 36, 143, 151
Circle of Fifths	38, 143
Code Division Multiple Access	134
coin problem	54
Constant Coefficient Equations	71
decimation filter	110, 142, 145
Delta Sigma Modulation	113, 114
determinant	80, 81, 82, 105, 141, 143
digital filter	117, 118, 119, 120, 121, 123, 125, 128
Digital to Analog Converter	110
Diophantine equations	45, 51
Discrete arithmetic	3
dual modulus prescalers	54
eigenvalue	81, 82, 83, 144
eigenvector	81, 82, 83, 144
Equivalence classes	9
error correction	136, 137, 138, 144, 147
Euclidean Algorithm	4, 5, 144
evenly spaced set	3, 7, 144
Factorization Theorem	39
Fermat's Last Theorem	55, 56
Fermat's Little Theorem	44
fifth	32, 33, 34, 35, 105, 143, 145
finite difference	59, 60, 61, 62, 67, 146
finite product	66, 67
finite sum	62, 63
flat	30, 36, 38, 145, 146
Frequency modulation	131
frequency ratio	31, 32, 33, 34
Frequency Response	103, 118
Frequency Warping	119, 120

Frobenius equations *54*
Frobenius Number *54*
Greatest Common Divisor *4, 5, 141*
half step *30, 37, 146, 151*
homogeneous equation *67*
Homogeneous Solution *46, 51*
hysteresis *112, 113, 147*
integers *3, 5, 8, 9, 11, 19, 45, 47, 52, 55, 144, 147*
IQ modulation *132, 133, 148, 149*
Jury's Stability Test *105*
Key Signatures *36, 37*
Laplace Transform *99, 100*
Least Common Multiple *6, 148*
Mandelbrot Set *93, 95, 148*
matrix *79, 80, 81, 82, 83, 84, 87, 105, 141, 143, 144*
method of undetermined coefficients *74*
minimum continuous divide ratio *54*
mod . *9, 11, 12, 13, 15, 16, 17, 19, 20, 21, 23, 24, 28, 29, 36, 37, 39, 44, 141, 148*
Morse code *129, 130, 152*
musical interval *31*
Nyquist Criteria *110*
octave *30, 31, 33, 34, 35, 36*
on-off keying *131*
oversampling *110, 111, 150*
parity check *10, 136, 150*
Particular Solution *46, 74, 75*
Pell's Equation *56*
phase modulation *132*
prime *4, 12, 13, 18, 23, 39, 40, 41, 42, 43, 44, 150, 151*
Primitive Pythagorean Triples *12, 55*
Pulse Width Modulation *112*
Pythagorean Triples *12, 55*
Quadrature Amplitude Modulation *133*
Quadrature Phase Shift Keying *132*
quantization *107, 108, 111, 115, 151*
quantizer *107*
Reduction of Modulus *19, 28*
Reduction of Order *72, 78*
root mean square *108, 151*
Sampling *107, 108, 109, 110, 115, 126, 141, 150, 151*
scale *36, 37, 147, 151*
sharp *30, 36, 151*
signal to noise ratio *107, 108, 110, 111*
square matrix *79*
telegraph *129, 130, 131, 133, 152*

Time Division Multiple Access	*133*
twin primes	*13*
Walsh functions	*134*
whole numbers	*3, 25, 51, 55, 147, 151*
whole step	*30, 37, 151*
Z Domain	*100, 101, 102, 103, 104*
Z Transform	*89, 99, 101, 102, 152*

www.ingramcontent.com/pod-product-compliance
Lightning Source LLC
Chambersburg PA
CBHW060852170526
45158CB00001B/323